William Wilberforce Newton

The Wicket-Gate; or, Sermons to Children

William Wilberforce Newton

The Wicket-Gate; or, Sermons to Children

ISBN/EAN: 9783337159672

Printed in Europe, USA, Canada, Australia, Japan

Cover: Foto ©Lupo / pixelio.de

More available books at **www.hansebooks.com**

THE WICKET-GATE;

OR,

SERMONS TO CHILDREN.

BY

WM. WILBERFORCE NEWTON,

AUTHOR OF "LITTLE AND WISE."

"Strive to enter in at the strait gate."—LUKE xiii. 24.

NEW YORK:
ROBERT CARTER AND BROTHERS,
530 BROADWAY.
1879.

Copyright 1875
BY ROBERT CARTER & BROTHERS.

CAMBRIDGE:
PRESS OF
JOHN WILSON AND SON.

ST. JOHNLAND
STEREOTYPE FOUNDRY,
SUFFOLK CO., N. Y.

PREFACE.

"The man therefore, looking upon Evangelist very carefully, said, 'Whither must I fly?' Then said Evangelist (pointing with his finger over a very wide field), 'Do you see yonder wicket-gate?' The man said, 'No.' Then said the other, 'Do you see yonder shining light?' He said, 'I think I do.' Then said Evangelist, 'Keep that light in your eye, and go up directly thereto, so shalt thou see the gate; at which when thou knockest, it shall be told thee what thou shalt do.' So I saw in my dream that the man began to run. Now he had not run far from his own door when his wife and children, perceiving it, began to cry after him to return; but the man put his fingers in his ears and ran on, crying, 'Life! life! eternal life!' So he looked not behind him but fled towards the middle of the plain."—*Pilgrim's Progress*

CONTENTS.

1. THE WICKET-GATE 9
2. THE EVIL MAGICIAN 43
3. LAMPS, PITCHERS, AND TRUMPETS . . . 71
4. RUNNING DISCIPLES 101
5. LEARNING TO THINK 125
6. SAMSON'S RIDDLE 153
7. RUNNING AGROUND 181
8. CARRIAGES TO JERUSALEM 207
9. THE FOURFACED CHERUBIM—1. THE FACE OF A LION 237
10. THE FOURFACED CHERUBIM—2. THE FACE OF AN OX 269
11. THE FOURFACED CHERUBIM—3. THE FACE OF AN EAGLE 295
12. THE FOURFACED CHERUBIM—4. THE FACE OF A MAN 321

I.
The Wicket-Gate.

THE WICKET-GATE.

"Enter ye in at the strait gate."—MATT. vii. 13.

AT the great Centennial Exposition at Philadelphia there were a number of little turnstile gates, by which people went into the grounds. These gates would only admit one at a time. Every time a person entered the gate clicked and registered the number of persons, and in this way, at the end of the day, by counting up the sum total of all the numbers of the register of the gates, the officers in charge knew just how many people had been admitted for the day.

But when the time came for closing the gates, the great fog-horn sounded, and then wide doors were thrown open on all sides, and the people within the grounds flocked forth by hundreds and thousands.

People entered at the *narrow gate*, and went out at the *broad way*. It would have been impossible for them to have gone in at the wide doors and come out at the narrow turnstile gate, one at a time. Each person who wanted to go into the grounds had to take his turn at the narrow turnstile gate. Every one was registered as they went in. Every one went in one at a time.

Now our Lord, in his Sermon upon the Mount, told those who were listening to him that they must seek to enter in at the strait gate, or the narrow gate. The word strait here means narrow. We say a person is in great straits, or is very much straitened, when he is crowded or pinched for money. The Straits of Magellan, or the Mediterranean Straits, are those places where the ocean, forcing its way through portions of land which lie near to each other, is very narrow, or strait, or straitened. What our Lord meant, then, by entering in at the narrow gate, or the strait gate, was, getting started right for heaven. *We must get started*

The Wicket-Gate.

right. We must begin in the right way. We must enter in at the right gate. And the right gate to begin the Christian life with, is the strait or narrow gate of obedience to the will of God.

When we go with the crowd, and please only ourselves, we are walking in the broad way. It is broad because so many people are in it, and because most people in the world suit their own pleasure and do just what they want to do.

But when we deny ourselves, and give up our wishes for the sake of God's will, or the happiness of others, then we are entering in at the strait gate. It may seem hard and narrow, it may crowd us somewhat, but this narrow way leads up after all to God, just as some narrow mountain path leads after a while to a broad summit, where we can see all our difficulties below us, and can feel so glad that we were not discouraged, but pushed boldly on to the top.

In Bunyan's story of "Pilgrim's Progress" Christian is represented as beginning his journey to heaven by entering in at the wicket-gate. Before this he had not been considered as fairly on the way to the Celestial City. When Evangelist told him what to do, as you can read in the preface to this book, he was tempted out of the way by Mr. Worldly Wiseman. Then Christian met his old friend and counsellor Evangelist again, who put him in the right way, and told him not to stop until he had reached the wicket-gate before him. After this we read that Christian "did address himself to go back, and Evangelist, after he had kissed him, gave him one smile and bid him God speed: So he went on with haste, neither spoke he to any man by the way; nor if any man asked him, would he vouchsafe them an answer. He went like one that was all the while treading on forbidden ground, and could by no means think himself safe, till again he was got into the way which he had left to follow Mr. Worldly Wiseman's counsel. So, in process of time, Christian got up to the gate. Now, over the gate there was written, 'Knock, and it shall be opened unto you.' He knocked, therefore, more than once or twice, saying,

"May I now enter here? will he within
Open to sorry me, though I have been
An undeserving rebel? then shall I
Not fail to sing his lasting praise on high."

The wicket-gate in this story means the same as the strait gate, or narrow gate, of our text. The word wicket comes from a Welsh word and means a little gate, or a gate of wicker-work, or lattice-work, such as we see in gardens, where there are chairs and gates and tables made out of pieces of rustic wood.

The wickets which boys use in playing cricket make a little gate, you know, with a small bar across the top. When the ball is thrown against these and tries to go through them, it knocks them down. The gate is so narrow that the ball can not enter it. It is a very little wicket-gate.

This entering in at the strait or narrow gate then means, as I have said, getting started right for heaven.

"Enter ye in at the strait gate," are our Saviour's words to all those who wish to have eternal life. This means that we must begin in the right way, we must get into the right path, we must get headed right for heaven.

Have you ever seen an ocean steamer back out of her dock and get headed right in the stream? Very often I see this done on a Saturday afternoon, when I go down Boston harbor with the tug which conveys the Cunard steamers out to sea. The steamer backs, slowly and carefully, while all the time the tug pulls away at a strong rope fastened to the steamer's stern, or puts its nose down against the great black iron side of the steamer, and roots at it until it has pushed it back and swung its stern out of the reach of the current, and then, when she is headed right, the tug stops all her puffing and blowing, and the big steamer gets under way and sails grandly down the harbor out to sea.

And it is not enough for us to *want* to

The Wicket-Gate.

get started right on our journey through this world to heaven. This life is like a great journey, and we must not only want to get to our journey's end; we must *do* all we can ourselves to get into the right path, and to enter at the right gate, just as the steamer tries, and the tug tries, and together they get headed right for the voyage.

"*Take nothing for granted,*" is a golden rule for all travellers. That is we must see things for ourselves, and find out all about our journey. We must not depend upon the opinions of others as to hours and trains.

I remember two boys, some years ago, in Philadelphia, who grew tired of going to school and minding their parents. So they made up their minds to run away.

They packed up their clothes, each one for himself, in a red silk handkerchief, and put their bundles over their shoulders, on a stick, in true pilgrim style, and sallied forth from the back gate of their father's house, very early on the morning of July 4th. They chose this day because they thought it was a good day on which to assert their independence. They thought they would be like the American colonies and would strike for freedom. So they went out to the West Philadelphia depot to take the train for Washington. It was in the war times, and they thought they would go and see President Lincoln. They wanted him to give them commissions in the army as drummer boys. They felt sure he would do this, for they had always heard that he was very kind. They thought he would invite them to dinner at the White House, and would very likely take them out for a drive in his own carriage.

So when they arrived at the railway depot they saw a train headed south for Baltimore, and they got on the rear platform. They had no tickets, and as they wanted to save what little money they had, they thought they would steal a ride to Washington. But the conductor found them out an hour after the train had started, hanging on to the steps on the rear platform. He landed them at the next place he came to, and lo and behold! it was Trenton, New Jersey. They were on the train to New York, instead of the train to Washington. They were going north instead of south; they had entered the wrong train, by the wrong gate, and were started all wrong.

So those boys who wanted to be so independent upon the Fourth of July, and strike out for themselves, like the American colonies, had the pleasure of spending their money in going home by the steamboat on the Delaware River back again to Philadelphia. And that very night at eight o'clock, just fourteen hours after they had passed out of their father's back gate, they passed in again, and went to bed. And their father, who was a very kind and wise man, let them have abundant time, for the next three days, each one in his own room, to meditate upon the great lesson of *getting started right* whenever we go on a journey.

And to this day those boys, who are now grown-up men, are very careful when they want to go to Washington to be sure and not take the train for New York.

For it is not enough to *want* to get started right; we must first find out for ourselves that we *are* right, before we go on our way.

You know the old motto says, "Be sure you're right, *then* go ahead!"

"Enter ye in at the strait gate;" or, as our Lord says in another place, "Strive to enter in at the strait gate"—the right gate.

Starting right for heaven. This is our subject to-day.

I.

First of all, then, we must find out what this strait gate is. It isn't the way that leads up to Mount Sinai, where the Ten Commandments were given. It isn't the Beautiful Gate of the Temple, where Peter and John healed the lame man. It isn't the gate that leads into the Church. Our Lord himself tells us what this gate is: "Then said Jesus, Verily, verily, I say unto you, I am the door of the sheep. All that ever came before me are thieves and robbers: but the sheep did not hear them. *I am the door:* by me if any man enter in, he shall be saved, and shall go in and out, and find pasture."

Again in another place he says, "I am the way."

Many years ago, in Switzerland, there was a great battle fought between the Swiss, who were trying to be free, and the Austrians, who were trying to conquer them. It was before the days of gunpowder. The Austrian knights were clad in steel armor and formed themselves into a solid square. This was called, in old times, forming a phalanx. Whichever way the Swiss patriots tried to reach their foes, there was this bristling front of spears, through which it was impossible for them to force their way. At last one of their number, seeing the utter uselessness of attempting to fight in this way, seized a dozen of the Austrian spear-points, and planting them in his own breast, exclaimed—"Make way for liberty." His companions rushed in over his dead body, and got inside the hollow square of Austrian knights and utterly routed them. This Swiss hero was named Arnold Winkelreid, and the battle is known in history as the battle of Sempach. Perhaps some of you may remember a piece which is often spoken on declamation days at school. It begins in this way:

> "'Make way for liberty!' he cried.
> 'Make way for liberty,' and died."

That was a very narrow way into the Austrian phalanx over the dead body of Arnold Winkelreid. When the sun set that day it set upon the happy and rejoicing Swiss, who were so glad to be free once more; but it also set upon the dead body of the one who died to make them free. He opened a way of escape for them from the tyranny of their enemies. But it was a very strait or narrow way: it cost him his life to make his country free.

And we sing sometimes in the Te Deum, or Chant of Praise to God,

"When thou hadst overcome the sharpness of death, thou didst open the kingdom of heaven to all believers."

Some time ago, here in Boston, there was a man who called himself a Christian minister, who said one day, from the pulpit, that it was time this idea of entering heaven by a trap-door covered with blood was done away with! What a dreadful thing to say! How else can we be saved but by the life and death of Jesus Christ? If there had been any other way of being saved would it not have been told us? If the law given upon Mount Sinai could have saved us, if the prophets or the apostles could have saved us, would not that have been enough? Where would have been the need of Christ?

But, my dear children, there are no words truer than those of that lovely hymn we sometimes sing. They are the very essence of the Gospel—the good news brought to us by Jesus Christ.

"There is a green hill far away
   Without a city wall,
Where the dear Lord was crucified,
   Who died to save us all.

"We may not know, we can not tell,
   What pains he had to bear;
But we believe it was for us
   He hung and suffered there.

"He died that we might be forgiven,
   He died to make us good,
That we might go at last to heaven,
   Saved by his precious blood.

"There was no other good enough
   To pay the price of sin,
He only could unlock the gate
   Of heaven, and let us in.

"Oh dearly, dearly has he loved,
   And we must love him, too,
And trust in his redeeming blood,
   And try his works to do!"

II.

Secondly, we must find out why this gate is so narrow. Why must we enter in at this *narrow* gate? Why must it be so strait?

"Enter ye in at the strait gate"—are our Lord's words.

My dear children, even Jesus found this way of submission to the will of God a strait or narrow way. Don't you remember he cried out in the Garden of Gethsemane, when he was all alone, and the disciples were asleep, and the glancing lights of Judas and the Roman soldiers were seen in the distance, coming along the road over the brook Kedron, "Abba, Father, all things are possible unto thee; take away this cup from me: nevertheless, not what I will, but what thou wilt."

It is always a hard or narrow way when we have to give up our own wills for the sake of another. This was why our Lord said it was so hard for a rich man to enter into the kingdom of heaven. It was hard for him to crowd down his will and enter in at the narrow entrance—the wicket-gate of obedience to God's will.

Last summer, when I was in London, I went to the great Zoölogical Gardens, and saw all the animals there. There were a lot of young elephants bathing in a pond. Presently the keeper ordered them out and marched them into the stable for the night. But there was one elephant which ran off by himself. He didn't want to go to bed yet. So he ran down the garden path, and all the people got out of his way. But presently he came to one of these same turnstile gates, such as they had at the Centennial Exposition. There the fellow stuck. He moved his head and trunk and his forelegs, and tried every way he could to get through the gate. But it was of no use: he couldn't crowd himself down. He couldn't manage it at all. He was like a camel going through the eye of a needle. And his keeper caught him and paddled him back with a long wooden paddle, on a trot home, while the poor elephant who would have his own way, kept his trunk up in the air and snorted and bellowed like a puppy dog when you spank him.

Well! we are all very much like this elephant at the gate. When we start out to have our own way at the beginning, though it may seem broad, *it's very hard to get through the narrow gate at the other end of the journey.*

Look at Benedict Arnold! In the beginning of the Revolutionary War he was a brave and true soldier. He fought in Canada, and had a good reputation for faithfulness and bravery. But, after awhile, he grew tired of his country's service. He thought he had not been treated rightly. He had his feelings hurt. He was jealous of attentions shown to his fellow-officers. His pride was touched. He grew very big in his own eyes, and presently he found that the path of obedience to General Washington, and those in authority, was becoming very strait or narrow. It crowded him. He was like Balaam on the ass, driven to the wall by the angel which blocked his way. There wasn't room enough for three in the road at the same time. He was like the elephant trying to crowd through the turnstile.

So you all know what he did! He jumped

over the wall on the narrow way of obedience to his country, and landed out in the broad way of disobedience, or of pleasing himself. He betrayed the forts on the Hudson, and fled in a boat to the British sloop-of-war Vulture, and became a British officer. But Washington arrived just in time to save the Highland forts, and nothing came, after all, of Arnold's treachery, save the death of poor Major André, who was hung as a spy. The way of his country's service was too narrow a way for Arnold, and so he became a traitor to his country, merely to please himself and have his own wishes gratified.

There was a country boarding-school once which was beautifully situated in the town. There were high walls all around the garden. But on one side the house joined on to the wall, so that from the windows one could see right down into the street below.

One week before Christmas, in a certain year, the boys saw written up in the large school-room these words, on a scroll:

> No Christmas Pies,
> No Frosted Cakes,
> No Weeping Eyes,
> No Pains or Aches.

Nobody could find out what this notice meant, until the day before the school closed for the term. Then the principal explained this motto. He told the boys that they could eat as many Christmas cakes and pies as they wanted to at home, but that they must not bring these things back with them in their trunks; since they made themselves ill with eating them, and then their parents blamed the teachers. So the boys promised, all but one of them, that they would try to do what the teacher wanted.

When the school opened again, after the Christmas holidays, the principal told the boys that he was sorry to say that he had some suspicions that they had not all complied with this new rule. He said that in order to be sure about this, two of the tutors would now examine their trunks, and mark them off in the way the custom-house officers did with the trunks of passengers from Europe.

There was one boy, named Ernest, who had told the other boys the day the school broke up that he meant to bring back a frosted plum-cake as large as a bucket. He said he wasn't going to mind any such ridiculous rule.

When he heard the principal say that the tutors were coming around to examine the baggage, he flew up into his room, locked the door, opened his trunk, seized his precious frosted cake——and then was wild to know what to do with it. He couldn't hide it in the closet, or under the bed; it wouldn't go into his bureau drawer; what was he to do? He heard the tutors coming; in a moment more they would be at his door. He flew to the window and looked out into the road. It was dark, but he knew there were some tall bushes growing up by the wall. "Rat-a-tat-tat," went the tutors at the door: down went the cake into the bushes!

"Come in," said Ernest, "I was changing my clothes."

Two sins in five minutes—deceiving, and then lying about it. That is the way in which one sin always leads into another. The tutors came in and examined Ernest's trunk and valise, and marked them with a big letter P, for "*passed*," and then went away. That night Ernest kept looking out of the window to see if he could find out any thing about his cake; and then he could not go to sleep—for thinking about it.

Early in the morning, as soon as it was light, he looked out of the window again. There he saw the big yellow parcel, tied up with the four pieces of red tape, just as he had thrown it down. It wasn't broken; it had lodged in the bushes. Now how was he to get it up? He mustn't make a noise about it, and he must get it up in his room before any of the school were stirring. Presently he saw a boy driving some cows to the pasture. Instantly he got out his fishing-line, tied the end of it on to his kite cord, and put on the fishhook a piece of white paper, on which was printed these words:

> HOOK THAT THERE BUNDLE ONTO THIS LINE AND I'LL GIVE YOU A SILVER QUARTER.

Ernest printed this message, for fear the boy might not be able to read it. The boy took it up, spelled it out, looked around for the bundle, while Ernest all this time was making signs to him, and pointing out where the cake was lying. Presently the boy found the cake and hitched it on to the string; Ernest pulled it up to his fourth-story window, just as if it had been a big blue-fish he was landing, and then wrapped up a silver quarter in a piece of paper, and threw it out to the boy.

So Ernest got his cake again. What was he to do next? Why, he must eat it; he must eat it all alone, for fear some of the boys would tell on him; and he must eat it up quickly, for fear the chambermaid or some one would find out that he had been eating a cake. So he began to stuff himself with this rich, black plum-cake. He ate it before breakfast and after breakfast, before dinner and after dinner, before supper and after supper, before he went to bed and after he was in bed. He wished now that his cake was smaller. He could not leave the crumbs around, he could not give it away, he could not hide it. The second night after eating the cake he was taken ill, and the doctor said he had been eating something that disagreed with him. Ernest would not tell what it was, but before very long the cake told the story itself, and the whole truth came out. Out of sixty-five boys Ernest was the only one who wouldn't walk in the narrow way of obedience to the rules of the school, and his sin found him out and told on him, as sin always does.

It is true what one has said on this subject: "If a man commits a murder, it seems as if nature sent a snow-storm on purpose, that his footsteps may be tracked."

Ernest was dismissed from the school for disobedience. He went on in the broad way of doing just what he wanted, going on from bad to worse, untill at last he joined some counterfeiters, and was arrested for forging a note, and served out his days in a penitentiary. And all this was because he was not willing to enter in at the strait gate of obedience. Truly does our Lord warn us about the power of our own evil hearts, when he said "Strive"—that is: try hard, try many times, again and again—"to enter in at the strait gate."

III.

And now, *lastly*. We are to find out why it is that we MUST enter in at this gate. Why can we not go to heaven by the broad way of sin? Why can't we go there by doing just as we please? Why *must* we enter in at this narrow gate?

Why did the angels rebel in heaven? Why did Adam sin in the garden? Why are our jails and penitentiaries filled to-day? Simply because it is so very hard to enter in at this narrow gate. It is so much easier to go with the crowd and do just as we want to do.

But just as surely as we must take the train south when we want to go south, and not the cars for the north when we want to go south, just so surely must we enter in at the strait gate of obedience to Jesus Christ, if we want to get started right for heaven! We must be like Christian coming up to the wicket-gate; we can not be fairly on our way to God, until we have put ourselves in the path which he has told us will lead to him.

There was a poor fellow in the slums of London who used to love to go to a certain dog-pit with his pet dog Tiger. The mans' name was Jonas Higgins. He was at times a good-hearted kind of man, but when a new dog was brought into the pit to fight Tiger, Jonas would bet his money on his dog, and then after the betting would come the drinking, and Jonas would go home as drunk as a fiddler. Tiger was a great fighter; one ear was gone, his upper lip was all torn away and showed his great white teeth, one eye was out, and his tail had been bitten off. All he had left was a bit of a stump, which he wagged like a drum-major's baton! Tiger was a good, kind-hearted dog. It was only in the dog-pit, when he was in his professional character as a fighter, that he was so fierce. He loved Jonas, and Jonas loved him with all the poor remains of his heart. Tiger came first in the love of Jonas, and then the wife and children came next. Jonas was known as "Tiger's man." Tiger was never spoken of as Jonas' dog. Well, it came to pass that right in the midst of this wretched place

THE WICKET-GATE. 37

where Jonas and Tiger lived together, a mission was established. The children of Jonas went to the school, and Jonas went to church, and before long Jonas became a changed man. Tiger was kept chained to his kennel; Jonas stopped drinking, and didn't go to the fighting pit any more. The home began to look clean and bright, and the poor wife was as happy as a queen. This went on for six months, when one Sunday the minister missed Jonas in church. After service the wife waited to tell the sad story. Jonas had fallen! His evil companions had tried in vain to tempt him back to the pit. At last they advertised that there would be a great dog-fight there, and that a big Scotch dog from away up at the north of Scotland would fight. It was said that this dog could whip any dog in England, since he had whipped Tiger. This was a lie. This was too much for Jonas. He had taken Tiger from his kennel and had gone to the pit. Tiger nearly killed the Scotch dog, and Jonas came home drunk. The minister went to see Jonas. He was very sorry for what he had done and promised to do better and he did. He went right back to his good ways and went steadily on for six months more. Then he fell again. This time it was a Dutch dog, from Holland, which it was advertised could whip Tiger. Again Jonas carried his dog to the pit, again Tiger whipped the other dog, and again Jonas came home drunk. This time he had the delirium tremens and was raving!

When he got well, the minister went to see him. He warned Jonas about this terrible temptation, and told him he must part from Tiger, or part from his Lord. He told him he could not serve two masters: that he must either deny his Lord, or deny the dog.

"Now," said he, "mark my words, Jonas. Take Tiger this very night, sew him up in a meal bag, and run with him to London bridge and throw him over, or else give up all hope of serving Christ any longer."

This was very hard for Jonas. He went out in the back yard to look at old Tiger.

The Wicket-Gate.

"Poor old fellow," said Jonas.

"Don't stop!" cried the minister.

"Dear old dog," said Jonas.

"In with him!" said the minister.

It seemed as if that minister never could get Tiger into the bag. His head would be out, or his stumpy tail would be out, as he backed his way out; and if Jonas hadn't kept talking kindly to him he would have killed the minister.

At last they got Tiger in. Then Jonas began to cry. He couldn't do it.

"You must," said the minister.

"I can't," replied Jonas.

"Yes you can," the minister answered. "Now then, there he is"—and lifting up the bundle—"there he is on your shoulder—now run!"

So Jonas ran, and the minister ran. Jonas cried all the way, and when he got onto the bridge he wanted to compromise.

"Let me sell him," said Jonas, "or let me give him away."

"No, sir!" said his friend, "you'll never

be safe while that dog is alive! So over with him—now then—when I say three over he goes—

"One!
"Two!!
"Three!!!"

What a struggle for poor Jonas! No one knew what it cost him, but he heard the splash in the water and ran home, crying like a child returning from a funeral! Parting from Tiger almost broke his heart, but it took the temptation away from him and saved his soul!

Now I call that—*throwing one's sin overboard.* It was indeed casting his sin behind his back, when Jonas consented to make such a sacrifice for the sake of his soul. Tiger was dearer to that poor, degraded sinner than any thing else in the world, and yet he parted from Tiger at the last, hard as it was to do so, when he felt that Tiger stood between his soul and his Saviour.

It was necessary for that man to enter in at a very narrow gate of sacrifice and obedience, if he wished to be saved. And he was strong enough to do it.

And so must we all, my dear children, give up our darling sins, and our pet habits, if they are in the way of our serving Christ.

We *must* head right for the kingdom of heaven if we are in earnest; and if there is any thing which is in our way, we must be willing to part from it, no matter what it may cost us.

Jesus said to cast away our eyes, or to cut off our arms, if they hindered us from entering into the kingdom of heaven.

He won for us eternal life by entering in at the strait gate of his Heavenly Father's will; and we must follow in his footsteps, for he himself has told us that the disciple can not be above his Master!

II.
The Evil Magician.

THE EVIL MAGICIAN.

"Woe unto them that call evil good, and good evil; that put darkness for light, and light for darkness; that put bitter for sweet, and sweet for bitter!"—Isaiah v, 20.

THIS sermon is about the evil magician and his hocus-pocus. Do you know what that word hocus-pocus means? If you do not, let us try and find it out.

Here we are, then, all of us, in a magician's room. There is the curtain, and there are the lights. Presently the bell rings, the curtain rolls back, and the magician comes forward upon the stage with a wand or rod in his hand, and begins to show us his wonders. Boys all love these tricks of magic, and there is a time in our history when we like to have magician's boxes, and do magician's tricks ourselves.

You all know what these tricks are. There is the wonderful egg-bag, and the hat out of which the flowers come; and there are the canary-birds, which are killed and made alive again; and there are the bowls of goldfish, which change places from one side of the room to the other. Then there are the wonders of second-sight, by which certain persons can be blindfolded, and yet can describe every article which is held up by another, though the eyelids are closed and the eyes are bandaged. Then there is the Indian basket trick, where a man gets into a basket and is locked down, and just when a second person is about to run a sword in the basket and apparently kill him,—when every one is breathless with astonishment and fear,—lo and behold! the man whom every one supposed to be in the basket is out in the hall, calling out, "What are you going to do?"

Now this whole world of magic is a wonderful world. And this word "hocus-pocus" is the old magical word which used to be spoken when any great trick was to be performed, or any great wonder was to be

The Evil Magician. 47

wrought. The magician would wave his wand over the place where the trick was to be made, and would make a long pow-pow, and say, "Hocus-pocus! hocus-pocus!" and in this way it came to pass that the word hocus-pocus was used for any thing which is intended to deceive us, or throw us off our guard, or play a trick upon us. Some people have said that this word comes from the Latin words "*Hoc est corpus*"—which are the words the priest uses in the Roman Catholic Church, at the altar, when the bread is declared to be the body of our Lord; when, according to their belief, this wonderful change takes place.

But, however this may be, we know that it is a very old word, and that the entire world of magic is a very old world. Look at the Indian jugglers, away off in India. For ages and ages they have performed their tricks, and they are perhaps the most wonderful tricks that the world has ever seen. These magicians don't require any stage, or lights, or trap-doors, or side scenery. They perform right on the grass, or on the sand, or wherever they may happen to be. I once heard a missionary from India, the Rev. Dr. Scudder, tell about these Indian magicians, and he said that in one of their performances they would take a little Indian girl, and lock her up in a basket, and instantly run a sword through the basket, in and out and every way, and that he heard her scream and saw the blood flow out of the basket, when—all of a sudden—ever so far back of the ring of people looking on, they heard a merry shout of laughter, and there stood the very little girl whom they supposed was dead. And then there are the Chinese and Japanese jugglers. They do the most wonderful things you can imagine. If you have never seen them there is no use in attempting to describe them. They throw knives at one another against a board, and make a rude image of a man out of the knives they throw that stick against this board. And they roll big barrels on their feet, and hold ladders on their chins, and men run up and

The Evil Magician. 49

down on these ladders. There used to be a company of these Japanese jugglers in the United States, with a little boy called "All-right." When he would do these dreadful things, and people would hold their breath and shut their eyes for fear of seeing him fall down and be killed, he would call out, in a shrill voice, after he had jumped, or got on his feet again, or landed on a rope, "All—right;" for this was all the English he knew; and so he was called little "All-right."

And then, too, we read about magicians in the Bible. The eastern countries used to be filled with them. We read about Moses, in the book of Exodus, having to deal with the Egyptian magicians who hung about Pharoah's court. When he went in before the king to show his signs and wonders, in order to induce him to let the Israelites go free, these magicians came up also and performed their tricks. When Aaron threw down his rod before the king and it became a serpent, we are told that the Egyptian ma-

4

gicians and sorcerers threw their rods down, and that they too became serpents. In St. Paul's second epistle to Timothy he speaks of certain men who were like "Jannes and Jambres," who withstood Moses. No doubt these were the names of some of these Egyptian magicians.

Then, further on in the history of the Israelites, we come across Baalam, who was a prophet and a great magician, whom Balak the king of Moab paid to curse the Israelites for his sake.

And we know that King Saul went, at last, the night before he died, to the cave of the witch of Endor, and King Manasseh consulted the wizards; and King Josiah banished them; so that all through the Old Testament we come across these magicians, who performed their tricks and deceived the people. We know, too, that Joseph before Pharoah, and Daniel before Nebuchadnezzar, interpreted the dreams which the astrologers and wise men were not able to do. And throughout the world's history these sooth-

The Evil Magician.

sayers and magicians have appeared from time to time to deceive people. Two hundred years ago people believed in witches, and many poor old women in England, and here in New England at Salem, were hung and burned as witches. And to this day there are gypsies who pretend to be able to tell fortunes, and magicians who perform wonderful tricks; only now we don't believe that they have any supernatural power; and though we may not be able to understand how they do these wonders, we know that they deceive us in some way, by what is called "sleight of hand."

And now we come to the subject of our sermon. It is this: the Evil Magician.

Do not these words of our text sound just like some great magician's tricks, the putting of one thing in the place of another, and then the "presto-change" of some wizard?

These are the words: "Woe unto them that call evil good, and good evil; that put darkness for light, and light for darkness; that put bitter for sweet, and sweet for bitter!"

Here then we have two great facts, and two great temptations. Let us take them in their order.

I.

And the first fact is this: *There is a real world.* We all know the difference between a real thing and an imitation of it. Here is a beautiful flower right out from the garden. It is a real flower, it has a rich fragrance, and we know that it is real. Here, on the other hand, is a wax flower or a feather flower. It is very beautiful perhaps, but it is not real; it is a false flower, only a beautiful imitation of a flower.

A great many hundred years ago, in Greece, there were three great painters. At last it was proposed that they should have an exhibition of their paintings, and that certain judges should decide which was the best of the three. After two of the painters had shown their works, they all came to see the painting of the third artist. At last, when they had waited for a long time before the curtain, and were wondering why it did not rise, they all cried out—

"Up with your curtain and show us the picture; don't keep us waiting here."

"That curtain," replied the artist, "is the only painting I have to show you."

The picture was so much like reality that the judges were deceived; they thought the false curtain—the merely painted curtain— was the real curtain. Now, my dear children, you know very well what this real world is in which you live.

You may not be able to define a tree, or a house, or a rock, or a horse, or a pond of water, but you know them when you see them. You can touch them all, and can say, "this is real, I have touched it; I know that it is real."

Why that was what St. Thomas tried to do with Jesus after the resurrection. He could scarcely believe that it was Jesus who was speaking to him. It all seemed too good to be true. He said, "Except I shall see in his hands the print of the nails, and put my finger into the print of the nails, and thrust my hand into his side, I will not believe." That is, St. Thomas would not believe it was Jesus who was said to have come from the grave again, until he should touch his Lord and find out for himself that he really and truly was alive. And just as we know there is a real world around us by touching and seeing and feeling it, so we know there is a real world of right and wrong within us, and that it is always wicked to mix these up, as the magician does when he deceives us with his hocus-pocus; and that it is always sinful to put evil for good, or sweet for bitter, or darkness for light.

And this brings us to the other fact of our subject. And that fact is this:

II.

Secondly: There is a false world. There are many things in the world which look as

The Evil Magician. 55

if they were real things, but are after all only illusions and deceits.

Some of the wonderful tricks of the magicians and wizards we were talking about a little while ago are called illusions, because they deceive us. There used to be a trick about a Sphynx's head, as it was called, which was an illusion. A man's head appeared on a cushion, and opened its eyes and mouth, and made all sorts of faces, and there was no body to it at all. It was only a head apparently cut off from the body, which did all this talk. But then we know the body *must* have been hidden by a looking-glass, or by some cover, and that people were deceived in some way by their senses.

There are very many things in the world, my dear children, which look real, but which are only, after all, imitations, and are false. A will-o'-the-wisp, for instance, is a false light, which often shines over marshy places and tangled swamps. Sometimes lonely travellers are deceived in the night by it, and follow on and on after it, hoping that they will reach at last this light, which seems to come from some house, while they are only trying to catch a shining vapor which goes before them all the time.

A mirage is another of these false things in the world. Sometimes on the sea-shore, or on the sandy plains of the desert, when the atmosphere is in a very clear state, some far-off trees, or rocks, or the houses of a distant city, seem to be enlarged and brought near; and sometimes rocks and trees and houses and steeples are reflected up in the sky, as if they were upside down. Many a time, at Rye Beach, I have seen the Isle of Shoals in a state of mirage; and very often, at Narragansett Pier, where I have written most of these sermons, I have looked over the water to Newport, and it has seemed like a fairy city reaching up into the sky, with all sorts of strange appearances about it.

There is one place in the Hartz mountains, in Germany, where travellers can go and stand on a certain mountain called The

Brocken, and can see their shadows reflected afar off in the morning sunlight, where they look like immense, great giants—something like the Titans of the old fables.

Now all these things in the world look as if they were real, but there is *a trick about them in some way;* they are illusions; they are false appearances. And just in this same way there is a false world within us. The right, the true, and the good come from God. "He is light, and in him is no darkness at all." St. John says in one place, speaking of these very falsities, or illusions, which were abroad in his day, and which were deceiving his converts, "Little children, keep yourselves from idols." That word idol means a false appearance, a deception; an image of God or of truth, not God or the truth itself. Our Lord, you remember, told us that Satan was the author, or the father, of all that was false and deceitful. "He is a liar, and the father of it," said Jesus. "He abode not in the truth, because there is no truth in him." He it was who brought sin and falsehood into the world. He it was who said to Eve, "Thou shalt not surely die," when God had said, "Thou shalt die." He made Eve believe that he was right, and that God was wrong. He made her think that the false world of deceit was the real world of truth, and that the real world of truth was only a false world. He was the first person who invented a lie. He was the evil magician who said, "Now I'll deceive the world, I'll trick them with my lies." He was the author and the inventor of this terrible change: this substituting the false world for the real world, this putting of evil in the place of good, and darkness in the place of light, and bitter in the place of sweet.

So now that we have discovered that there are these two worlds,—the real world of nature and the false world of nature,—and have found out that these two worlds are also reflected in our own souls, so that we can tell by our conscience, evil from good, and light from darkness, we come to the two great temptations which are brought to bear upon us all.

I.

The *first* temptation is when the devil tries to make us believe that the *false* world is the *real* world.

See how hard he strove with Eve. Wherever God had said "Thou shall," he said "Thou shalt not"; and wherever God had said "Thou shall not," he deceived her with the words "Thou mayest."

Now, my dear children, for myself, I believe that it is this great Father of Lies going about, as St. Peter says, like "a roaring lion seeking whom he may devour," who makes it so hard for people to obey God and do right. Here is God's word from heaven; here is Jesus Christ, once in the world to save it; here is the Christian Church, the very sheepfold our Saviour built himself; here are the records of God in human history, and the marks of the Creator in the rocks, and the touches of the Holy Spirit of

God in our spirits, just as the breath of a player is heard and felt through a flute; here are the promises of the Bible, and the commands which Christ himself has given; and yet, in the face of all this truth, Satan, the Father of Lies, comes to us men, women, and children, through our evil thoughts, and says, "Tush! tush! it's all a lie. There is no God. Eat and drink, for to-morrow you die."

Now isn't all this just like the magician who says, "Now you see something, and now you don't. Hocus-pocus! Presto-change! Every thing is changed."

Where does all this doubt about God come from? Where does sin come from? How is it that this world is so very evil? Why is it so hard to do right and to keep from doing wrong? Ah, my dear children, these questions have perplexed the bravest souls in the world's history. Many men have wondered and questioned and doubted, and have tried in every way to find out an answer. But there is only one answer, and it is this: there is a lower world of sin and darkness;

The Evil Magician.

how it has come we know not, but from that dark world of deceit and evil, sin, like some contagious disease, has arisen, and our natures are set on fire with it. We get the habit of lying and deceiving from him who is the Father of Lies. He is the great seducer or destroyer of souls. He makes men believe that the false world is the real world, and the real world is the false world. As St. Paul says, in one place, through his power men are given to believe a delusion. In Bunyan's story of "Pilgrim's Progress," you remember, he is called Apollyon the destroyer. When Christian came into the Valley of the Shadow of Death, or, in other words, when any of us are overcome by our doubts and fears, then Satan, or Apollyon, comes to destroy that Christian altogether. If we can only be influenced by the devil to give up our faith in God, and to do just as we want, and never think of the future world, or of the judgment to come, then he has performed his tricks in our hearts just as he wants to do, and we make this world every thing, and "jump the world to come."

Evil takes the place of good, darkness takes the place of light, bitterness takes the place of sweetness; and God writes out with his own hand, just as the man's hand appeared before the frightened Babylonian king and wrote his doom, that black and heavy word—woe!

Woe to him who confounds right and wrong! woe to him who changes truth into falsehood! woe to him who turns good living into evil living!

II.

And then there comes the *second* temptation, when we are led to believe that *the real world is the false world.*

Some years ago, in England, there was a great actor named David Garrick. People crowded to see him act; he made every thing seem so real. Men and women would cry over the sorrows that he seemed to have when he acted upon the stage, and would

The Evil Magician.

listen to every word he said and watch every thing he did.

One day a minister, who knew him very well, said to him, "Garrick, how is it that people go to see you play at the theatre, and won't come to hear me read the Bible and preach?"

Garrick was silent a moment, and then said: "Do you want me to tell you what I think is the true reason?"

"Yes," replied the minister, "that is just what I want."

"Well," said Garrick, "you have to do with real things, and I have to do with imaginary things. But you, by your unreality, make the people think that your real things are imaginary things, while I throw myself into the play, and make the people think that my imaginary things are real things."

There was the whole matter. The minister wasn't real enough. The people didn't believe in him, because he didn't seem to believe himself in what he was preaching.

Now I know, my dear children, how hard

it is always to believe those things which we do not see, but which are nevertheless real and true. We are caught by lies; we are taken by surprise every now and then. Look at Simon Peter in Pilate's Hall. All of a sudden a great temptation was sprung upon him, and his Master and his words weren't real enough to him, *just at that moment*, to save him from tumbling down into falsehood and denial. All his old faith went in a moment; it all seemed unreal. The servant-maid and the soldiers seemed to be the real world, and his Jesus Christ, his old Lord and Master, seemed to be unreal; and so he fell.

And in this same way we fall into temptation when it comes upon us. We forget about the inner world in which God is, and see only the outer world where man is; and so God's real world is forgotten in the presence of the world that now is, which seems to us the only real world.

You know we live on the surface of the earth. We dig down and come to water and rocks. We don't see these rocks; they are under us and are hidden. But there they are, under the earth's surface; and there couldn't be any surface, if there wasn't any underground interior.

Or go with me and look at the wonderful Brooklyn Bridge, over the East River, in New York. There those two gigantic piers stand! Steamers and ships sail under the wire bridge, and the wires of the bridge rest on those great granite piers. It's very wonderful indeed! But what do those heavy piers rest on to support the wires of the bridge? We can't see any thing; they seem to grow up out of the ground. Or look at the great tower of Trinity Church here in Boston. It seems to rest upon the roof, and it looks as light and graceful as if it was made out of pine wood. But down in the cellar of that church there are heavy granite blocks, taken from the old Trinity Church, on Summer Street; and these blocks of stone are piled together, and four heavy piers rest upon the granite foundation, and the beautiful tower, which every body sees, rests after all upon the old granite blocks which no one sees, but which are hidden and buried in the cellar, away out of sight.

Well, my dear children, just what the earth's interior is to its surface,—just what the heavy, unseen foundations are to the Brooklyn Bridge and to the great tower of Trinity Church,—God, and his truth, and his righteousness, are to this world. He can not deceive us; that is the devil's work, not God's work. He has planted in our nature this idea of right and truth; it has all come from him, and though we do not see these foundation-stones of our character, because they are hidden in our souls; there couldn't be any character at all without them: just as there could be no surface of the earth without an interior, and no bridge or tower without the foundations—real, though unseen—for them to rest upon.

David says, in one of his psalms, "If the foundations be destroyed what shall the righteous do?"

If we say there is no right and truth, if we hocus-pocus with right and wrong, if we put evil for good, and darkness for light, and bitterness for sweetness, and mix them up so that we can not tell the false world from the real world,—as the magicians do with their tricks and illusions,—where will we be, and what shall become of us?

But there *is* a true world and a false world; there *is* such a thing as light, and it is from God; and there is such a thing as darkness, and it is from the devil; and we must learn to keep ourselves from idols,—from falsities and wrong conceptions,—and to know good from evil, and darkness from light, and sweetness from bitterness, and never—never—to do the devil's work, and put the one in the place of the other.

And now we are through.

Remember these two facts of our sermon to-day:

1st. There is a real world, and
2d. There is a false world.

And remember the two temptations which come to us all:

1st. The temptation to believe that the false world is the real world, and

2d. The temptation to believe that the real world is the false world.

And, above all, remember that black word —woe!

Oh how dark it looks! It is God who speaks it by the voice of his prophet. It is not an idle word. God means what he says.

The whole world will go wrong if we trifle with God's standards of right and wrong. It is like trifling with a clock which governs a railroad, where hundreds of trains move by it! It is like trifling with a compass on a ship at sea, by which the vessel's course is steered! The trains may run into each other if the clock in the superintendent's office is wrong; the ship may be dashed upon the rocks if the compass is altered.

And souls may be lost, and the world be ruined, if we trifle with God's standard of right and wrong; if in our studies, our work, or our play, we say, "It makes no difference how we live;" and if, like the Father of Lies, we mix up right and wrong, and put "evil for good, and darkness for light, and bitterness for sweetness."

Remember this text to-day, then; and when you trifle with truth or with righteousness, remember God's word, sounding like a peal of thunder and saying, "*Woe unto you!*"

III.
Lamps, Pitchers, and Trumpets.

LAMPS, PITCHERS, AND TRUMPETS.

"A trumpet in every man's hand, with empty pitchers, and lamps within the pitchers."—JUDGES vii. 16.

THESE words are found in the story of Gideon. We ought to know all these Bible stories at once, when we hear any reference to them, without having to go and read about them; just as in school we ought to know our Latin Grammar rules without having to go to the book every time we are called upon for a rule.

In old times, before there were so many books, in the old cathedrals and churches in Europe, the architects would cover the walls and the windows with paintings and stained glass and mosaic work, representing all the old Bible stories. St. Mark's Church, in Venice, is covered all over with Bible pictures in this way, made in mosaic work—or the process of putting little colored stones together so as to make a picture. In this way it happened that though many of the poor people could not read the Bible, there was the open Bible before them all the time; so that they couldn't help seeing and knowing a great deal about it.

Now the story of Gideon is this: Once upon a time, in a very rough period of the history of the Israelites, before they became a nation and had a king,—when they were in the long promised land of Canaan very much as the early colonists here in America were before the colonies became the United States, when the French used to come down in incursions from Canada, and the different tribes of Indians attacked the settlers here,—the surrounding nations, the Midianites, and the Moabites, and the Jebusites, and the Hivites, and all the rest of them, were in the habit of fighting with the Israelites.

About the year 1245 B. C., or 2,490 years before 1245 A. D., the Midianites, who lived to the east of Canaan, came down upon the new settlers there and tried to drive them out. There was no king in those days among the Israelites, and no regular standing army; but here and there were chieftains, or judges, as they were called, something like the old Scottish lairds and chieftains we read about in Sir Walter Scott's "Tales of a Grandfather." They would raise a company of men from their district, and other companies would join them, and in this way they would get together quite an army. Othniel was one of these warlike chieftains. He drove back the Assyrians, and for forty years was the judge or dictator. Ehud was another deliverer. He was a rough, wild, unscrupulous man. He assassinated the king of Moab, and drove the Moabites back to their own land. Shamgar was the name of another of these chieftains. He killed six hundred Philistines with the club he used for goading his ox in his ox-cart. He must have been a rough sort of judge to those who were on the opposite side. Then there was Deborah, a prophetess, who used to go out to battle with a great military captain named Barak. They defeated Jabin, king of Canaan, at that time when Sisera was killed by Jael, the woman who thought she was doing right in telling a lie and deceiving an old friend, but who did a wicked, cruel thing after all.

Samson, the strong man and the great mischief-maker, was another of these judges, and he plagued and tormented the Philistines until they got hold of him, and put out his eyes and cut off his hair, and took all the strength away from him. Abimelech and Jephthah and Gideon were also leaders of the people, in their different hours of trouble. Eli and Samuel were the last of the judges, and after them came the kingdom, with Saul as the first king.

Well, as we were saying about Gideon, the Midianites came swarming down from the East upon the Israelites, and brought their families and cattle, and took possession of the land, and ate up all the provisions. It was a regular invasion. The Midianites came as

LAMPS, PITCHERS, TRUMPETS. 77

conquerors of the land, and it looked just as if they meant to stay. At last the Israelites became so poor and downtrodden that it seemed like their old days in Egypt, when they were the slaves of Pharaoh. So they took to praying for deliverance, for people generally pray in earnest when they are in trouble; and God at last raised up Gideon, and inspired him to become their deliverer.

So Gideon raised an army; and then, for fear there were too many men in it who might have said, "We gained the victory ourselves, with our own hands," he resolved to make his band smaller. First, he told all those who were afraid to go out to battle that they could return home. And twenty-two thousand men accepted the invitation and went home. I suppose they made all manner of excuses. Some of them didn't feel very well, and some of them had their feelings hurt because they hadn't been made officers, and some of them were in favor of compromising with the Midianites by making peace with them, and some people didn't like Gideon's way of fighting: he made them march out in the open plain, while they liked, above all things, to get behind stone walls and fences. So they went home, shaking their heads about poor Gideon and pitying him!

There were ten thousand men left who were ready and willing to go to the battle. But God told Gideon there were too many yet. So Gideon brought them down to a brook, and told every man to drink. Then there was a strange scene. Some of the men got down deliberately upon their hands and knees, as if they were playing camel, and put their mouths down to the water, and took a long and very comfortable drink; just as some of us may have done when we were out fishing on some of our rivers and lakes. They enjoyed themselves, and had a good long drink, and took their time to it. Others of Gideon's company were in such a hurry to go after the Midianites, that they wouldn't take the time to get down upon their hands and knees, but lapped the water up to their mouths by their hands. "These are the men for me," said Gideon; and he sent all those home who did not lap up the water; and nine thousand seven hundred men went back again, and Gideon was left with only his three hundred men.

Then that night, in the black midnight, Gideon took his servant-man with him, whose name was Phurah, and he stole over to the Midianites' camp. There were their camp-fires and their tents; he could hear the horses neighing and stamping in their stalls, and could see all that was going on. Some of the soldiers were sleeping and snoring, and some were playing games, and some were eating and drinking, and others were telling stories. We read that "the Midianites and the Amalekites and all the children of the East lay along in the valley like grasshoppers for multitude; and their camels were without number." What a scene this must have been to Gideon and his man-servant, as they crawled in and out over the rocks and among the trees. Presently he heard one of the soldiers in the tents telling a dream he had, about a loaf of barley which tumbled into the camp and knocked down a tent. Then another soldier said, "I'll tell you what this is: this is the sword of Gideon, for into his hand hath God delivered Midian." This was enough for Gideon. He turned to go back to his three hundred brave men, but first we are told he worshipped. This means that before he went back he knelt down and thanked God for what he had heard.

Then he divided his band into three companies, and instead of giving each man a sword, or a shield, or a spear, we read "he put a trumpet in every man's hand, with empty pitchers, and lamps within the pitchers." After this, when the word of command was given, these three companies rushed into the middle of the camp, breaking their pitchers, and waving their torches, and blowing with their trumpets, and shouting, "The sword of the Lord and of Gideon." Of course a panic followed, just like that which happened to the Assyrians at the time when King Hezekiah was invaded; the Midianites took to fighting each other, and a perfect rout ensued. Gideon and his men drove them out of the land altogether, and killed their princes. We read about this in the 83d Psalm, where the psalmist, in speaking about the enemies of his country, says: "Make their nobles like Oreb and like Zeeb: yea, all their princes as Zebah and as Zalmunna." These were the names of the Midianite princes whom Gideon destroyed.

After this all the people, of course, wanted to make Gideon king, but he declined the honor. But the people never forgot about Gideon's band, and his wonderful battle with the lamps, pitchers, and trumpets. They remembered the deliverance, just as we remember the battle of Lexington, or Bunker Hill, and talked and wrote and sung about it, along with the stories of the Passover night, and the conquest of Canaan, and the forty years in the wilderness.

This is the story of Gideon. Now we want

to find out what lesson the lamps, pitchers, and trumpets teach us.

Well, my dear children, the one great lesson for us is this: we must learn to fight life's battles with the weapons God has given us.

These men in Gideon's band didn't complain because they couldn't have shields and spears and swords. It was God who was fighting for them and protecting them, and they were safe in his hands. He knew best what would make their enemies afraid; for when people are afraid they always run. Look at the siege of Jericho! Instead of bringing great battering rams and engines and catapults to knock down the walls of that city, God told Joshua to let the priests go around the city for seven days blowing rams' horns! How the Jericho-ians must have made fun of the priests! I suppose they walked around the walls imitating them and laughing at them; but by and by, when the time came, sure enough, according to God's word, down came the walls as flat as a pancake!

There are two ways of fighting: one is by arms, and the other is by strategy, or the way of taking your enemy by surprise. And there are two modes of warfare: one is by attack, and the other is by defence. When a city is stormed, as Yorktown was stormed by Washington and Lafayette in the Revolutionary War, or when Sebastopol was taken, in the Crimean War, there are men called sappers and miners, who dig approaches to the besieged city, and throw up earth-works, as they get nearer and nearer, to defend the attacking party.

There is a motto which says, "Every thing is fair in war." This isn't true; but then it's very hard to know what is right when we have got into such a state that we think it is right to kill off as many of the enemy as we can. Right and wrong get fearfully mixed in war times, and cannon smoke makes it very cloudy in the conscience.

There have been some generals who were famous for deceiving their enemies, and then killing them when they were tricked. Hannibal, the great Carthagenian general, was one of these men. He used to deceive his enemies, the Romans, and beat them by his tricks and strategy, or generalship. One time he let a part of his army fight the Romans and then he brought around in their rear a great quantity of elephants, which waved torches over their heads with their trunks. The Romans had never seen elephants in this way, and they were frightened out of their lives, and ran like a herd of scared sheep.

But this battle of Gideon's with the lamps, pitchers, and trumpets, was to make the Israelites feel that they were dependent, after all, upon the God of their fathers, who had always taken care of them from the day when they left Egypt all the way down to their day. The battle was won not by their skill in fighting, but by their obedience to God and their trust in him.

And, my dear children, there are hidden enemies all around us, as there were around the Israelites in Canaan. They are in reality worse than these Midianites and Moabites and the others which were around God's chosen people. If we are Christians, we are trying to drive out these evil habits and temptations from our soul, just as Joshua and Gideon and these other chieftains drove back the enemies that came settling down upon them and occupied the land. God has given us our weapons as he gave them to Gideon, and if we are to win in the great fight of life we must use them as Gideon's band did, when they shouted out, "The sword of the Lord and of Gideon."

Lamps, Pitchers, and Trumpets. What do these three weapons mean?

I.

First of all come the Lamps. "Lamps within the pitchers."

These lamps were not glass lamps or lanterns; they were very probably torches made out of long sticks with pitch and tar and turpentine on the end. If you have ever been in the woods, camping out at night, you know how easy it is to cut a club, and tie pine cones on to the end of it, and use it as a torch. I suppose these lamps were torches, or flambeaus, something like the kind we use in the woods.

Three hundred of these flaring torches in the dead of night would make a great light.

A torchlight procession, you know, such as we have before our elections, makes a great show at night.

Well, whatever these lamps were, they were hidden for a while in the earthen pitchers or jars, and then, when the time came to flare them aloft, down went the pitchers and up went the lights!

In other words, our lesson is, if we want to win, we must use our light and knowledge; we mustn't keep our lamps hidden in the pitchers. Now you know we all have this light of truth within us! Some of this light is in the world of Nature, some of it is in our own hearts, and a great deal of it is in the revelation of God's word from heaven.

We sing in one of our hymns—

LAMPS, PITCHERS, TRUMPETS. 87

> "Let the lower lights be burning,
> Send a gleam across the wave."

This means that we must not shut up our light and truth to ourselves, but that we must let others know of it. Our Saviour's words are, "Let your light so shine before men, that they may see your good works, and glorify your Father which is in heaven." And David says, "Thy word is a lamp to my feet and a light to my path."

Look at the moon in heaven! What makes it so beautiful? Simply the fact, that instead of taking in or absorbing all the light of the sun, it reflects it and gives it forth to us! Use your light, my dear children: use it for yourself, use it for others.

I remember a story of a deacon who used to pray, "Oh Lord! bless me and my wife, and Uncle John and his wife—we four, and no more!" That man hadn't got his lamp out of the pitcher! He wasn't waving it aloft for others to see by. On the other hand, there was Paul Revere, in the old tower of Christ Church, here at the North end!

When he saw the bonfire that told about the British coming, he got out his lantern and hung it up, as a signal for all the people in Boston. Why Beacon Hill, where the State House now stands, was in old times a place where a great blazing bonfire or beacon was made to be seen down the Charles River and the harbor. That is what its name comes from. And in the same way, my dear children, we ought to be lights and examples to others of the light that we have within us.

"Jesus bids us shine in this dark, dark world:
Jesus bids us shine:
You in your small corner,
    I in mine,
Jesus bids us shine."

We oughtn't to act as if we didn't know the difference between right and wrong, and truth and falsehood. We oughtn't to act as Chinese or African children act, who don't know any thing about Jesus Christ! We are in the light; we have had the light and truth given to us by Jesus our Saviour; we have been brought up in the Christian

Church, we ought to wave our lamps aloft for others to see by.

There is an old Greek motto, which is represented by a hand giving a burning torch to another hand, and underneath are these words:

"Λαμπάδια ἔχοντες διαδώσουσιν ἀλλήλοις."

"Having lights they pass them on to others."

That ought to be our motto, if we are followers of God as dear children.

II.

Secondly, come the Pitchers. These pitchers were very probably large earthen jars, or stone barrels, something like those which were meant for holding water at the marriage feast at Cana of Galilee. Gideon's company used these pitchers or jars as a dark lantern, to keep their torches in. Perhaps they had rosin and turpentine in them, to help make a flame. These pitchers were of great use up to a certain time, but after that they were only in the way. There was a time to use these pitchers, and a time to break them. Of course they made a great clatter when three hundred of them were shivered into bits upon the ground, and in this way they helped to frighten the Midianites. But their first use was as receptacles, or boxes, to hide the lamps in, until the time came to use them. They were made to be used, and then to be broken when the hour of their use was passed.

And here we find out the meaning of these pitchers. They held the lamps up to a certain time and then they were thrown away, because they were no longer of any use. So it is with us: there is a time to use our lantern holders, and a time to throw them away. By the pitchers, or lantern holders, then, I mean all those things which help us to retain our knowledge and light. I mean books and rules, and plans and resolutions. All these things are of great use to us up to a certain point; they are like the pitchers which held the lamps; but after all it was the lamps which did the work on the Midianites, not the pitchers. My dear children, you have all got to learn that you must hold your own torches in the world, and fight your own way against the trials and troubles and temptations in your path. There is a time when you must take your lamp out of the pitcher, with as much fire as it has got on it, and must throw your pitcher away. I mean by this, that there is coming a time when you will have to act for yourself: you won't be able to lean upon your parents, or your friends, or your teachers, or your books. You will have to act for yourself, according to the light you have; and that is just like the moment when Gideon's band threw aside their pitchers and went for the Midianites.

In other words, and here is the point of the whole matter: you must get out your light and knowledge from books and friends and parents and the whole outside world, and you must *get it into your own head.*

I remember a man in college who used to draw lines of geometry—squares and cubes and triangles—on the blackboard, and then, when he came to explain them to the professor and the class, he would say, when the professor said,

"How is that, Mr. ———?"

"That's what the book says, sir; that's what the book says."

That man was holding on to his pitcher: he wasn't using his own lamp one bit. The book was necessary to get the idea into the man's head, but after it was there it was of no more use. But the trouble was that the man didn't get the idea into his head at all! He was like one of Gideon's men who would want to keep dipping his lamp in his pitcher all the time.

There was a general in the late war for the Union, who was a citizen brigadier-general. He was a dry-goods merchant, and he raised a lot of money and some men, and they made him a brigadier. He went to work and bought some military books, "Mahan's Field Fortifications" and "Marmont's Spirit of Military Institutions," and studied these at night.

At last the day came when he met the enemy in battle. He had his books by his side, and his maps on his saddle, and while the battle was going on, he was looking through his spectacles, up and down his book, to see what he should do next. At last a big shell came and burst near him, and it made him feel bad, and he had to leave the field; and it is needless to say his army was all broken up.

That miserable brigadier-general was holding on to his pitcher, when he ought to have been waving his lamp! He should have known what to do next, at the front of the attack, *out of his own head*, instead of studying in the rear rank, out of his book.

Cortez, the conqueror of Mexico, knew better than this brigadier-general. When he landed on this continent, and saw that his followers kept an eye on their ships, in which to return in case they were beaten; he did a grand, bold thing: he burned his ships, so that his men had to fight hard to win, in order to be saved.

You know there is an old expression about

"Throwing away one's scabbard." That simply means that there comes a time when the sword only is of use, and that its sheath, or the receptacle which held it, will never be wanted any more. And just in this same way we must learn to use our books and our knowledge until we have got possession of them, and then we must learn to walk ourselves, without using crutches all the time.

I remember a minister once, who said he could write sermons well enough, but his only trouble was a want of ideas. Now there was nothing to be done with that man: he hadn't any lamp himself; he was hugging on to his pitcher; he was depending upon books and rules, and all sorts of outside things; he was afraid to throw away his pitcher. He wouldn't count *one* in the battle-field of life!

III.

And then, *lastly*, there are the Trumpets. You know what a peculiar note that of a trumpet is. It is harsh and shrill; it can be heard at a great distance and sounds like a fog-horn at sea. Whenever you see a procession of soldiers, and hear a band of music, you can always hear, above all the other instruments, the sound of the trumpet. There was a blind girl once, whose teacher was trying to explain to her the different colors. After she had explained to her blind pupil the color scarlet, she asked her what she thought it must be like. "Oh," replied the blind girl, "I think it must look something like the way a trumpet sounds." That was a most excellent definition of a trumpet. Now these shrill trumpets in Gideon's band were used on purpose to frighten the Midianites. In the dark night they saw the lamps waving, and heard the pitchers break, and above all this stir and noise they could hear Gideon's men blowing away on their trumpets.

Now then, just as the lamps mean knowledge or light, and the pitchers represent the means by which we receive or carry our light, so the trumpets mean the sound of the human voice—speaking, talking, and asking questions. We can't get on in the world without talking. Even the poor deaf and dumb people have a sign-language of their own, and talk to each other by means of their fingers.

The trumpet means for us, in this story, the sound of the voice: it is the power of uttering our thoughts to the world by the means of language.

There was a little girl once, who left her home in the country to go on a long journey to Boston in the cars. Some of the family were afraid to have her go alone, but her old, queer Uncle Hugh thought it was best for her to go. So they all gave her bits of advice. One said, not to jump off the cars while they were in motion; another said, not to put her head out of the window; a third said, "Sit in the middle of the car"; a fourth said, "Give your ticket to the conductor"; a fifth said, "When you arrive at the depot, take your first turn to the left, then your second to the right, then your third on your left, etc.";—and the poor child had so much advice given her that she was afraid to start off. But her old uncle said, "Polly, my dear, instead of giving you advice now, I only give you this note. After the train has started, open the note and follow the advice. Good-by." So Polly started off. After she had bidden them all good-by, and had wiped her eyes and was comfortably seated in the cars, she thought of her Uncle Hugh's note. So she got down her bag and opened it, and took out Uncle Hugh's letter. It read as follows:

"DEAR POLLY:—Here are my rules for travellers. Mind them and all will go well.

"Your uncle, HUGH."

RULES FOR TRAVELLERS.

I. Do as other people do.
II. Take nothing for granted.
III. Use your bell-clapper.

The bell-clapper was the tongue. What Uncle Hugh meant to say to Polly was, "Use your tongue: ask questions." And, my dear children, the tongue is one of the greatest weapons for good or for evil in the world. Out of it cometh blessing and cursing, words of prayer and words of sin. When wrongly used it is a terrible weapon for evil; but when we use it rightly it is as great a weapon to bear down falsehood and destroy ignorance as Gideon's trumpets were the weapons by which the tents of the Midianites were tumbled down.

Lamps : Pitchers, and Trumpets.
Seeing : *Holding* : *Speaking*
Light : *Self-reliance* : *Communication.*

These are the three weapons in the soul's warfare against sin which we must use, *each in its right way*, if we would win in the fight against evil and temptation, as Gideon won in his battle, by using the weapons God told him to use. We must pray to God, through

Jesus Christ, to help us to get our outside knowledge into our soul, and to let it shine for him, just as Gideon's band had their pitchers first, and their lamps afterwards; and we must pray to him to help us to use our voices in his cause, and on the side of the truth, as Gideon's men did, when they waved their torches and sounded their trumpets and cried, "The sword of the Lord—and of Gideon."

IV.
Running Disciples.

RUNNING DISCIPLES.

"So they ran both together: and the other disciple did outrun Peter."—JOHN xx. 4.

THERE is always something the matter when grown-up people run. Boys and girls hardly ever walk — they always run. But men and women very seldom run. All young creatures love to run. Look at a basketful of kittens, or a box in the barn with puppies; or look at calves and lambs in a pasture. They are running all the time; round and round they go spinning about, and never stopping to rest, till it is time for them to go to sleep. And when we are children we seem very near to the little animals, and love to read about them, and see pictures of them, and play with them or with toys which represent them. We are young animals ourselves when we are little, and we play and scamper and cut up capers just like the lambs in a field. And then as we begin to grow older we become more quiet and sedate, and one of the first things which marks the difference between the man and the boy, and shows us that the boy has become the man, is that he *walks* now instead of *running*. Running belongs to boys; walking belongs to men. So, as I was saying when I began, there is always something the matter when people run. If there is an accident in the street, or a dog-fight, or a man being arrested, or a procession of soldiers, or a lightning calculator, people will run as fast as boys. Then, too, people always run when there is a fire, or when they have to catch a train or a steamboat, and haven't much time.

Here in Boston, where we live, a great many people have their homes out of town and come into the city every day for business. A great many boys and girls come in town to school in the early trains, and go out to their homes after two o'clock. I have often watched people hurrying to the cars, as

Running Disciples. 105

I have waited at the Brookline depot. All along the streets leading to the station the people keep coming, looking up at the station clock, and at last, as the minute hand points to one minute of the hour, every body runs,—men, women and children,—and those that are fast catch the train, while the laggards have to wait for the next train. Now in the words of the text we have an account of a race between two disciples, to see who should get first to the sepulchre where their Lord had been laid. It was Peter and John who ran together to the tomb. St. John does not tell us that the "other disciple" was himself. But then we know perfectly well that it was St. John who always spoke of himself as the "other disciple." He did not like to use the pronoun "I." He was very humble-minded and did not like to talk about himself. Just remember this, my dear children, and when you talk and write, see how many times you can blot out the word "I," or can get on without it in conversation, and you will be all the better for it.

Well, to come back to our story, on the first day of the week, or the day after the Jewish Sabbath, Mary Magdalene, the woman whom our Lord had healed and forgiven, came running into Jerusalem with a wonderful story. She hunted up Peter and John, and told them that she had been to the tomb of Jesus, and that he was not there. She was afraid some one had stolen him. "They have taken away the Lord out of the sepulchre," she said, "and we know not where they have laid him." You see Peter and John had not been to the sepulchre yet. Peter had kept away by himself ever since the moment when he denied Jesus in the Judgment Hall, and had gone out in the early morning to weep bitterly. St. John had been with the mother of Jesus at the foot of the cross, and had taken the poor, heart-stricken Mary home again, and had, in all probability, been with Joseph of Arimathea and Nicodemus, in carrying the body of the dead Christ to the tomb. In the cathedral at Antwerp, in Belgium, there is the famous picture by the painter Rubens, of the Descent from the Cross. Rubens was one of the most celebrated painters in the world, and this is his greatest painting. It is a wonderful picture. Joseph of Arimathea is there, and Rubens has put St. John in the picture. He is receiving the cold and lifeless limbs of the crucified Saviour, and you can see how gently and tenderly he is taking them into his arms. But whether St. John was present when Jesus was buried, according to this picture, or not, he had not been to the tomb since the Sabbath day. Therefore, when Mary Magdalene came running in and saying that Jesus was not in the sepulchre, Peter and John went right out with Mary, while it was yet early in the morning, and walked rapidly to the tomb. Then, I suppose, when they came near to it they began to run both together, and as they went on running faster and faster, John who was probably lighter and more active than Peter, got ahead of him and outran him and came first to the tomb. But there he stopped, and waited for the others to come up. He stooped down and looked into the cavern of the rock and saw the linen clothes lying there, but he did not go in. Then when Simon Peter came along, he did not stop at the door of the cave; he went right in and took notice that the head napkin, which had been on the Saviour's brow, was not with the rest of the grave-clothes, but was wrapped up and put in a place by itself; showing that some living person had been there. Then the "other disciple," as St. John called himself, went into the sepulchre and he saw and believed. Then Peter and John went home again, but Mary, faithful Mary, the first at the tomb in the morning and the last to leave it, remained in the garden, and was the first person to whom our Lord showed himself alive on the morning of the Resurrection. On another occasion, when our Lord showed himself to the disciples on the Sea of Tiberias, after his resurrection, John was the first to see Jesus upon the shore, but Simon Peter threw himself out of the boat and was the first to land.

So St. John did not always outrun Peter, although he did when they ran their race to the sepulchre on the first Easter morning.

"Running disciples." This is the subject of our sermon to-day.

What do we learn from it?

I.

First of all, we learn there are some disciples who have come to a stand-still. When people go to Europe in the great ocean steamers, which go back and forth so regularly between Europe and America, they never think about the machinery, which is stowed away in the vessel's hold, until it stops working, and then every body is awake and on deck, to know what is the matter. Sometimes the long shaft which turns the propeller has to be screwed up, or keyed up, as it is called; and to key up the propeller the machinery has to be stopped, and when the machinery stops and the steamer comes to a stand-still every body begins to wonder about the machinery, though they never thought about it before. It is the same way with a train of cars when they stop suddenly and there is no station in sight. The windows go up, and people's heads go out, to see what is the matter, what is the reason for this stand-still. And when the machinery of the human body is affected, and some parts of it stop working, or work slowly, then we begin to wonder what is the matter with us. Sometimes we never know we have a head till we have a headache; or never know that we have a heart or lungs until they need keying up, like the propeller at sea, and we have to drop our anchors, and furl our sails for a while, and get rested. There are a great many of these stoppages in life. Some people stop being respectable. Boys and young men who loaf around street-corners, and taverns and engine-houses, have come to the stand-still of respectability. Other people stop being honest: they don't pay their bills, and don't care for their good reputation of being thought upright persons. They need keying up in their morals. And then there are a great many people who were once running disciples of the Lord Jesus Christ, who don't even walk in his ways any longer. They are disciples who have stopped following him, they have come to a stand-still. And then, just as with the steamer and the locomotive and the sick person, where there is something wrong, you may depend upon it there is something the matter with these persons' souls. There are many people who get into such a state of mind that they don't believe in any God, or any soul, or any future. They don't think that life is worth living, or that there is any use in being good or in doing good. Now, my dear children, I tell you it's a dreadful thing to get becalmed in this way, and become disciples who have come to a stand-still, — disciples who don't go at all!

There is a very pretty song, which some of you may have heard, about a clock that wouldn't go. One verse of it is as follows:

"My grandfather's clock was too large for the shelf,
   So it stood ninety years on the floor;
It was three times as large as the old man himself,
   But it weighed not a pennyweight more.
It was bought on the morn of the day that he was born,
   And was always his treasure and his pride;
But it stopped—short—never to go again—
   When the old man died!
Ninety years without slumbering, tick—tick—tick—tick;
His life's seconds numbering, tick—tick—tick—tick—
It stopped, short, never to go again,
   When the old man died!"

Well, my dear children, there are a great many Christians in the world who are like a stopped clock. *They don't go any more.* You can't tell the Christian time of day by looking at their faces. Something's the matter inside. Why look at the early Church at Jerusalem, when they were waiting for the Spirit of God to come down upon them! When Jesus died, the disciples seemed to stop going, like this "Grandfather's Clock." After his resurrection, and ascension into heaven, they waited at Jerusalem for the day of Pentecost to come, but they had many doubts and fears, you may depend upon it, about the future. No doubt James and Andrew thought of their old fishing haunts on the Lake of Galilee, and Philip wondered about his friends and companions at Bethsaida, and Levi remembered his past life as a collector of taxes. The entire Christian Church had come to a stand-still. Much of their faith and hope had stopped, and if the Church had sprung out only from man, it would have never gone on again, like some old and rusty clock that was all worn out.

But when the Spirit of God came down upon them like flaming tongues of fire, the Church which had come to a stand-still went on again, and the old companions of Jesus became running disciples in his service once more. It was just like fresh steam coming to an engine; it was like a fresh breeze striking a becalmed vessel; it was like keying up the steamer's shaft, or like winding up a clock which had run down. And when we feel that we have come to a stand-still, when our faith has stopped, and we don't take any pleasure in serving Christ or in praying to him, then we ought to ask the Holy Spirit to come to us with fresh impulses and desires, to enable us to go on in his service again. For we will never in the world get to heaven if we are only disciples who are standing still.

II.

Secondly: There are *some disciples* who are *walking* disciples. We hear a great deal in the Bible about a person's "walk and conversation." You know we can very often tell a person's character by his handwriting, and by his way of walking, and by the tones of his voice. When Simon Peter denied his Lord in the Judgment Hall, the maid-servant said that she knew he was one of the followers of Jesus, because his speech betrayed him. It had the Galilean accent, just as we can tell a person who comes from Down East, by the tones of his voice. If a person has a short, mincing step it shows that his character and his will have influenced him so that his very gait partakes of this peculiarity. When a man rolls and lounges as he walks, and swings his shoulders from side to side, like an old sailor ashore, or a jolly old elephant in the menagerie ring,—we know that the man is a good-humored, kind-hearted soul. There is a great deal, after all, in a person's walk; and thus it happened that the Apostle Paul got into the way of speaking of the Christian's *walk* and conversation. A drunken man's walk and conversation reveals a drunken man's character. He staggers and swears, and we know at once what kind of a man he is. We would be very much surprised to see a minister, or a church deacon, reeling along the street and swearing. That would not be the walk or the conversation for those who professed to be the followers of Christ. When people go to a funeral they walk in slow and solemn procession; they don't run, or hurry the body to the grave. But when we see any person whom we love very much, and whom we haven't seen for a long time, we generally hurry up our steps and run to meet them. After our Lord's resurrection he overtook two of his disciples as they were going to a little village called Emmaus, and they walked together. The disciples did not know that it was Jesus. As they walked along the road our Lord explained the Scriptures to them, and then, when they arrived at their journey's end, they asked him to remain and eat bread with them. And we read that "they said one to another, Did not our hearts burn within us, while he talked with us by the way, and while he opened to us the Scriptures? And they rose up the same hour, and returned to Jerusalem, and found the eleven gathered together, and them that were with them, Saying, The Lord is risen indeed, and hath appeared to Simon. And they told what things were done in the way, and how he was known of them in breaking of bread."

Don't you suppose that those disciples hurried back over the way they had come with quicker steps, because they had seen their risen Saviour, than they did when they were slowly walking out to Emmaus? It makes a great difference, I tell you, in our walks, what motives we have which are leading us. I knew a boy once, who was so slow, and who used always to be late at school, and to play, and to every thing except dinner, that we boys, who used to play with him, called him "Sergeant Slowboots." You know boys very often give good names. And to this day, whenever I meet that man, there he goes, sauntering along as if there were twenty-seven days in the week instead of seven; and I believe still, that nothing but his dinner ever makes Sergeant Slowboots hurry up. If we are going to the dentist's we generally take our time to it. We are not in a great hurry to get there. But if we are going out into the country to have a good time, on Saturday afternoon, in October, we don't like to waste the minutes on the way by walking slowly. In China, on the great rivers there, there are many boatmen who keep great quantities of ducks and geese in their boats, or junks, as they are called. In the morning a plank is let down from the side of the junk, and the ducks and geese go off for the day, to swim about and pick up what they can get on the water. Then at night they come back to the junk and wait until the plank is put down for them to get on board. Then what a hurrying time there is! They jump and scramble and flap with their wings, and beat one another back, for the last duck always gets a whipping. There stands the Chinese boatman with his whip of three cords; and woe betide the last duck, for she catches it thick and fast. So those ducks don't stand still or walk on the plank. They run up into the boat as fast as their waddling web feet and their wings will carry them.

Well, my dear children, if we are really trying to walk in the way of God's commandments, we ought to be eager and ready to walk according to his laws. We ought to pray the prayer of the psalmist, "Quicken thou me in thy way," so that we may be able to say: "I will run the way of thy commandments when thou shalt enlarge my heart." God doesn't expect hard things of us; he does not ask us to do impossible things for him. But just as we ought not to loiter on our way when we have been sent on errands by our parents, and just as it is unnatural and shows that there is something wrong when we don't want to meet our father, and don't want to walk home towards our father's house, so, as the disciples of Jesus, we ought not to lag along in his service, and be sleepy, tired, stumbling disciples, ready to halt every little while, and not caring very much how fast or how slow we are going.

We may not all be able to be great saints, running towards Jesus all the time as Peter and John ran to the sepulchre, but there will be a blessing for us in doing what we can for Christ, even that blessing which attendeth him who "walketh not in the counsel of the ungodly, nor standeth in the way of sinners, nor sitteth in the seat of the scornful."

III.

Thirdly—there are running disciples. We have seen what kind of disciples stand-still disciples and walking disciples are. Now we come to the last set, or to those who are running disciples. Some of our Lord's disciples get on faster than others. We read in our text that "the other disciple did outrun Peter, and came first to the sepulchre." John was ahead of Peter all the time. He saw things before Peter did. He had a quicker eye and a quicker step. You know how this is. Some people when they enter a room see every thing that is in it right off, while other people never seem to notice any thing at all. Some people are lithe and active, and can run for a chair or a book, while the rest of the company are wondering what to do. It is this quick eye and quick step which makes a business man

Running Disciples. 121

successful. Never to be above one's work, never to think any little action too little, to be always ready and willing for service, these are maxims which will make busy, promising boys in stores and offices successful and enterprising men.

When he was a young lieutenant, the officer in command asked the Duke of Wellington, then known as Arthur Wellesley, how soon he could leave London for India. The Duke of Wellington looked at his watch and replied, "In fifteen minutes, sir." And sure enough, in fifteen minutes there was the duke at the door, with his small trunk on the carriage. Now I call that quickness and readiness which the Duke of Wellington showed, the sign that he was a *wide-awake*, running disciple of his country. He *ran to do his duty*, as Peter and John ran to the sepulchre. He did not loiter on the way, or walk slowly, or come to a standstill like the steamer in mid ocean, or the old "Grandfather's Clock." God's angels in heaven are running disciples. They fly to do his will. Nothing stands in their way.

> "God builds on liquid air and forms
>   His palace chambers in the skies,
> The clouds his chariots are, and storms
>   The swift-winged steeds with which he flies.
>
> "As bright as flame, as swift as wind,
>   His ministers heaven's palace fill.
> They have their sundry tasks assigned,
>   All prompt to do their sovereign's will."

When a person runs he must have some object in view which influences him to take such quick steps. In a yacht-race or in a horse-race, those who do the driving are urged on by the desire of winning. Every possible inch of canvas is put upon the boat, and every available pound is taken off the wagon, to insure success. And St. Paul, in his first Epistle to the Corinthians, says: "Know ye not that they which run in a race, run all, but one receiveth the prize? So run that ye may obtain. Now they do it to obtain a corruptible crown; but we an incorruptible. I therefore so run, not as uncertainly; so fight I, not as one that beateth the air: but I keep under my body, and bring it into subjection: lest that by any means, when I have preached to others, I myself should be a castaway." St. Paul was a running disciple. He said he was the weakest of the apostles, and was not fit to be called an apostle, because he had persecuted the Church; but nevertheless he outran all the other apostles, and was the most wonderful man that has ever appeared in the Christian Church.

Children, I want you all to be running disciples of Jesus; eager and ready to be doing and living for him. Don't stand still. Don't saunter along in the way of duty as if it didn't matter much what time of day it was when you got home. Be quick-eared, quick-eyed, and quick-stepping in the service of your Master, as those two disciples were when "they ran both together, and" when "the other disciple," that is the one who loved his Lord the most, "outran Simon Peter"—the man who had denied him—"and came first to the sepulchre"; that empty sepulchre where Death had been robbed of his sting, by the Saviour of the world, on the world's first Easter Morning.

V.

Learning to Think.

LEARNING TO THINK.

"And it came to pass, that after three days they found him in the Temple, sitting in the midst of the doctors, both hearing them, and asking them questions."—St. Luke ii. 46.

WE all know this story about the boy Jesus with the doctors in the Temple. It is the only glimpse we have of our Saviour's child-life.

There are many stories about the life of Jesus as a boy which are untrue, and which read like the stories of the "Arabian Nights" and all such Eastern tales.

But although we have read this story of Jesus with the doctors so many times, let us to-day go over it once more, and see just what it was and what it teaches us.

The caravan or company of worshippers who had come down from the hill country of the north to Jerusalem, were on their way back again when Mary and Joseph first missed their boy. There were no stages, or any means of travelling, in those days, over this journey. It was seventy miles from Jerusalem to Nazareth; about as far as from Boston to Springfield. Some of these people went on foot, and some were on mules, and some were carried in carts and wagons. They travelled together, so as to be protected from any robbers or wild beasts; and at night they would pitch their tents and light their fires, to keep themselves warm, and to frighten off the jackals.

It must have been like a great picnic; and the children, no doubt, enjoyed these trips to Jerusalem very much. First, there was the great city to see, with all its wonders. Think how these country boys and girls must have enjoyed seeing the Roman soldiers, and the horses and chariots of the nobles, and the great palaces, and the Temple, with the priests and the people there. Then think, too, how they must have liked going back with the caravans, running along the line and playing with each other; and how they must have enjoyed gathering sticks for the fires at night, and snuggling to sleep under the tents; for there is always a fresh feeling in going to sleep for the first time under a tent. I suppose that Joseph and Mary were talking with their friends about the Passover Feast, from which they were just returning, when some one said, "Where is your child; where is your boy, Jesus?" and Mary replied, "Oh, he is in the company somewhere, with the rest of the children!" But by and by he couldn't be found. The other children were all there—all the Nazareth boys and girls. But none of them could tell any thing about Jesus; none of them remembered seeing him. "Where did you see him last?" asks the frightened Mary, getting her things together to go right straight back for him. Some of the children thought they remembered seeing him talking with the old doctors in the Temple when the caravan started out, but they weren't sure about it. No one ever is sure about a thing when it's lost you know, but after it has been found then they are always sure they were right. Well, Joseph and Mary left their friends in the company, bound home to Nazareth, and they posted back in haste to Jerusalem, to find Jesus. First they looked all through the caravan to see that he was not there. We read that "supposing him to have been in the company they went a day's journey; and they sought him among their kinsfolk and acquaintance." This means that they went up and down the line, looking in among all the groups of children for their boy. But he wasn't there, and so they had to go all the way back to the city. First of all, I suppose, they went to the house where they had been staying; but he wasn't there. Then they inquired in the streets, but none of the watchmen had heard of any lost child. And then, after three days' search, they went to the Temple; and there, in one of the side-rooms, or nooks, they saw a group of old men leaning forward around their darling boy, while he was hearing them talk and was asking them questions.

Learning to Think. 131

What a scene this must have been! There were the old men crouching around the child when the door was opened, and there stood Mary and Joseph. "Son,"—she said,—"why hast thou thus dealt with us? behold, thy father and I have sought thee sorrowing." There was some rebuke in these words for Jesus: as if she had said, "Why have you given us all this trouble? We have been searching all through the caravan and all through the city for you."

The words of Jesus in reply to his mother were wonderful words, and made a deep impression upon her mind. The others which were about her did not get the meaning of them, but his mother remembered all his words, and kept these sayings in her heart. For Jesus told his mother that it was now time for him to be about his Father's business; and that must have reminded Mary that Jesus was beginning to find out who he was, and what he had to do in the world. It must have carried her thoughts away from their quiet home life in Nazareth, to the great mission which the angels had announced Jesus was to undertake: and his mother, who had been thinking only of her life at home, and bringing up her child there, must have been awakened to the true idea of the life of her boy who was, even then, beginning to feel that he must learn all that he could, so as to get to work about his Heavenly Father's business.

Learning to think. This is the subject of our sermon to-day.

This picture of the child Jesus sitting among the doctors, hearing them, and asking them questions, is the picture of every true boy and girl who wants to know what the truth is, and who wants to be of some use in the world, and be about our Heavenly Father's business, as Jesus was.

I do not mean then, at this time, to speak more about this story of Jesus with the doctors. We might spend all our time in studying out the lessons of this scene. Though Jesus was the Son of God he had a human soul and a human mind in a human body, and he had to grow in wisdom as well as in stature.

And thus it comes to pass that at twelve years of age we see him beginning to grow: we see him learning to think. We watch him putting his foot on the first round of the ladder of knowledge, we find him "in the midst of the doctors, both hearing them, and asking them questions."

I.

First of all, then, if we would truly grow in wisdom as we grow in stature, and would learn to think for ourselves, we must know how to *ask* questions. Perhaps you may think, my dear children, that it is unnecessary for any one to tell you this; that you constantly hear them at home saying, "Oh, don't ask so many questions!" But then you know there was a time when your parents and teachers did just this same thing.

There was a class once at school which

kept asking the teacher so many questions that at last he said, after scolding them, "Boys, I wish you would remember that this is a *school* and not a *debating* society." So the boys made up their minds that they would not ask another question. The recitations went on like clock-work. Any boy who asked a question was sure to be punished for it by the other boys at recess-time, and for a whole month the teacher wasn't asked a single question about geography, or arithmetic, or the history of Eneas in Virgil. At last the teacher laughed out in school and said, "Well, boys, this is worse than the other. You've got some conspiracy against me; never mind what I said a month ago, ask me all the questions you want to." And the boys were right. We must ask questions.

The only way to travel is to take nothing for granted, but to keep on asking questions! And what is this life of ours, after all, but a journey, a travelling along over a path which our fathers have trodden before us?

"We are travelling home to God
In the way the Fathers trod:
They are happy now, and we
Soon their happiness shall see."

Some time ago I asked a ferryman whom I knew, at one of the slips in New York, to let me stand behind his window, where no one could see me, on purpose to hear the questions the people asked who came down to the boat.

Here are some of the questions:
"What time does the 7.15 train start?"
Ans. "At seven-fifteen!"
"At seven-fifteen?"
"Yes, ma'am!"
"Jane, he says it goes at seven-fifteen."
"Well, ask him when it arrives."
"Say! man! halloo there!—hi! what time! look here! what time does it arrive?"
"Arrive where?"
"Why, arrive at Trenton!"
"9.30."
"Nine-thirty, Jane."
"Well, ask him if he thinks it will be on

time; and ask him whether we had better wait, and if there *isn't* any earlier train; and ask him if he saw a man go through here with a baby wrapped up in a red shawl."

"Halloo there! ticket-agent! Hi!—He won't answer me. How impolite some men are. I say! Look here! Man! Here! I want to ask you something!—say!—Did you see?—there now; he's talking to some one else."

Now that is really about what I heard behind the window, only there was ever so much more of the same kind than I can tell you.

"How do you stand this life?" I said to the ticket-agent.

"Stand it!" he replied. "Why I stand it as eels stand skinning; I get used to it. But only think," said he, "what we would all be saved if people only knew *how to ask questions.*"

Now that is the point. We ought to learn how to ask questions. We must not ask foolish questions, or questions which we could easily answer ourselves, if we would only stop to think about them. We mustn't want to have our minds *carried upstairs all the time;* we mustn't be lazy, and get into the way of having other people think for us. We must think over our questions, and not trouble people to answer questions which we are too stupid or lazy to think out for ourselves.

If that woman at the ticket-office had only thought that the 7.15 train must leave at 7.15 o'clock, she would have saved one question at least.

So, then, I believe, my dear children, in asking questions. Jesus did it when he was a boy, with the doctors in the Temple. Only I believe in knowing *how* to ask questions, and in stopping to collect our wits over what we are about, and in learning to think over our questions.

For the only way to know is to seek to know: "Ask, and ye shall receive; seek, and ye shall find; knock, and it shall be opened unto you."

It is wonderful, when we come to think about it, to find that the interrogation mark, this question idea, stands over so many forms of knowledge. You find it in your games and plays, in your enigmas and rebuses and conundrums, in your arithmetic with its puzzling questions, and in algebra and geometry and logic. Why do these games and studies ask all these puzzling questions of us? Why do they make us stop and think? Because they are designed to teach us how to think; and if we would learn how to think rightly we must know how to ask questions.

II.

And then, *secondly*, if we want to learn to think we must know how to answer questions.

It's very easy work to ask questions, but sometimes it is hard work to answer them.

Some children say, when they want to give a good reason for any thing, "Because." "Because what?" "Why, because." Now just to say "Because," is no reason. That

Learning to Think. 139

isn't any answer at all. Away over in India some of the old philosophers, in describing the earth, said that it was a plain and that it rested upon a great elephant. But the people asked, "What does the elephant rest upon?" "Oh," replied the philosophers, "the elephant stands upon an immense turtle." "Yes," said the people, "but what does the turtle rest upon?"

The philosophers didn't know this: and so they said that the turtle didn't rest much upon any thing. Now that wasn't answering the questions which the people put to them. It was just like the children saying "Because," when they hadn't any reason to give.

My dear children, it is a great thing to be able always to give a good reason for our course of conduct or belief.

When the old patriarch Jacob was dying, he called his sons to his bedside to give them each a father's blessing. It was a difficult matter to find out a good character to some of these men. The most of them had been hard-hearted, cruel boys. When he came to bless Naphtali, all the old man could say was this: "Naphtali is a hind let loose: he giveth goodly words." A hind let loose! Did you ever see a heifer tumbling about in a pasture lot? They prance about and whisk themselves all over the field, making the barn-fowls fly around and disturbing the sedate old cows, bothering the sheep and making the horses look up from time to time to see what they are up to. Well, that is the way many people act and talk; their tongues get loose and they wag like a heifer, or a hind let loose in a pasture lot; they give goodly words as far as the sound goes, but there isn't much sense to what they say.

St. Luke says, in his account of the child Jesus talking with the doctors in the Temple, that "all that heard him were astonished at his understanding and answers."

And so, if we would learn to think, if we want to grow in wisdom as we grow in stature, we must know how to answer

Learning to Think. 141

rightly quite as well as how to ask questions rightly.

"Johnny," said one little boy to his fellow classmate in Sunday-school, "I would have been afraid to have gone up in that chariot of fire as Elijah did. Wouldn't you?"

Johnny thought a while and then said, "No, Tom; not if I knew that the Lord was driving those horses."

That was a good answer.

St. Peter says, in one place in his first epistle, "Be ready always to give an answer to every man that asketh you, a reason of the hope that is in you, with meekness and fear." And St. Luke, when he wrote his gospel to Theophilus, said that he did it on purpose that he might "know the certainty of those things" in which he had been instructed.

It is a great comfort in life to be able to make a good answer, and to think before we speak.

When the Dutch were in possession of New York, when it was New Amsterdam, before it had been taken by the English, old Wouter Van Twiller, the governor, went to inspect one of his forts. When his vessel anchored before the fort, and his flag was dipped to salute it, he was in a great rage, because the commander didn't return his salute by firing off his guns in honor of his distinguished visitor! So he sent for the commander, and demanded of him how he dared to show his superior such an insult. The poor commander gave twenty reasons why he failed to fire a salute. He didn't know that the governor was coming, he hadn't men enough to man the guns, and then, last of all, as his twentieth reason, he said he "*had no powder.*"

Now if that poor old Dutch commander had known how to give a good answer, he would have given his *twentieth* reason *first*, and then there would have been no need for the other nineteen.

Knowing how to answer questions, is the second way of learning how to think.

III.

Thirdly: If we want to learn how to think, we must be willing to know more.

He that is willing to learn will be able to teach, but he who says, I know enough already, can never expect to grow. I remember a fable about some mice who lived in a barn. The little mice heard the big mice talking about the dreadful farmer's boy and those awful creatures the dog and the cat. But they had never seen any of them. They never went away from home; they lived all the time in the old grain box away up in the hay-mow; and after a while they got very careless and didn't believe there was any thing to be afraid of. At last one of them strayed away from home and got lost. All of a sudden the cat ran after her, and the dog chased the cat, and the farmer's boy threw a big stone at the dog; and the poor little mouse ran for its life, and just got home in time to save itself; but ever after that it believed that the world was a very large world, and that there were a great many things to learn, of which it had been ignorant before.

And it is a very large world, my dear children, and if we are unwilling to learn, or if we think we know enough already, we will not grow in wisdom as we grow in years, in the way the boy Jesus did, when he was so eager to find out from the doctors in the Temple all that they could tell him.

There was a great lawyer in England once, named Sir Edward Sugden. People wondered how he could remember so much, and why it was that he always knew the right point of law for the case in hand. One of his friends once asked him the secret of his success, and this was his answer: "I resolved," said he, "when beginning to read law, to make every thing I acquired perfectly my own, and never to go to a second thing until I had entirely accomplished the first. Many of my competitors read as much in a day as I read in a week; but at the end of twelve months, my knowledge was as fresh

LEARNING TO THINK. 145

as on the day it was acquired, while theirs had glided away from their recollections."

We must want to know more, and we must try to know more, if we want to learn how to think. Remember this, my dear children. Learning how to think rightly, is the way to learn how to act rightly, for "as a man thinketh, so is he."

There are two bad habits which keep us back from knowledge. They eat into our character just as moths eat into a garment. One of these bad habits is "Didn't think," the other is "Don't care."

"Oh, Willie! Willie!" said his mother to a little boy who was sent to the apothecary's with a prescription, "where have you been? What have you been doing? You have been gone three hours."

"I didn't think," said the boy; "I waited to see the Firemen's Procession."

And all that time his poor little sister was growing worse with the disease, and the medicine which ought to have been given at once was too late, and the poor child died.

"*Didn't think*," killed Willie's little sister. Oh! but we ought to think; we ought to learn to think; we ought to know enough to teach us to think. We ought to tie a millstone around "Didn't think," and drown it in the depths of the sea. Dear children, don't get into the habit of saying "I didn't think." Suppose the engineer of a locomotive was to say "I didn't think," when he was looking out of his window and driving his engine; suppose the doctor should say "I didn't think," when he wrote the prescription; or suppose the druggist wasn't to think, when he made up the medicine; or the carpenter wasn't to think, when he built the house; what would become of us all? People *must* think: men and women must think, captains of vessels must think, generals in a battle must think, we must all think about what we are doing; it won't do to say, "I didn't think."

Therefore, we must begin to think while we are children: we must think about the questions we ask, we must think about the answers we give, and we must try to know more day by day.

The other bad habit which keeps us from wanting and trying to know more, and which eats into our characters like a moth in a blanket, is "Don't care."

What is to be done with a man who don't care for any person, place, or thing,—who don't care for himself, or his friends, or his family, or his God,—who don't care about his soul, or sin, or the hereafter?

Every time I look into a pig-sty and see the great lubberly hogs lying deep in the mud, and rooting their noses in the swill-trough, I say to myself: "There are the fellows who don't care." What do they care for appearances, for decent habits, for a good clean reputation? What matters it to them what you think of them? *They don't care* for any thing but food and mud. They are the true "Don't-care" fellows.

Some time ago there was a man who failed in business, and who was arrested for forging a check. He was tried in court and sentenced to the state's prison. One of his old schoolmates went to see him in the court the day he was sentenced, and spoke to him as he was getting into the prison van along with the other prisoners. "Poor fellow," said his friend, "I am so sorry for you, Jones."

"Oh," replied Jones, in his seedy clothes, "I don't care."

"And this,"—said his friend when he was telling the story to some others,—"this was just what he used to say when he was kept in and flogged at school, when he was set down at the tail of his class, and when he 'flunked' over and over again, and was sent up to the principal and was suspended. He always used to say 'I don't care,' and the boys called him 'Don't-care Jones.'"

Dear children, remember these two dreadful habits, which keep you from increasing in knowledge,—these two big moth-millers which will eat into your character,—and have nothing to do with "*Didn't think*" and "*Don't care.*" They will surely keep you back from wanting to know more. You can not grow in wisdom as you grow in years if you *don't think* about things and *don't care for* them.

IV.

There is one other thing we must do if we want to learn to think rightly; it is this: we *must wait to know more.*

I remember when I was a small boy at school, first studying my Latin Grammar, that it used to look very hard over towards the end of the book. I used to wonder how I would ever be able to understand it, with all its long sentences and big words and heavy rules, that looked like lead. But I had to wait till I got there before I could understand it. And we must all learn to wait, in order to know some things, because we can not understand them now.

A father takes his little boy to see some machinery. He shows him the boiler and the piston-rod and the walking beam and the steam-chest, and then the little fellow says: "But tell me how the fire and the water makes the wheels go around." The father tries to tell him about the steam, and the opening and shutting of the valves, but the little fellow can not understand it. "But how does the steam make the wheels go around?" he asks again. And then the father says, "My dear child, I can not explain it to you now, you will have to wait until you have learned more; then, when you are a big boy, you will understand it."

And just in this same way Jesus said to his disciples, "I have many things to say unto you, but ye can not bear them now:" That is, the disciples were to wait until they had gone up into a higher class, until they had been taught more by the Spirit of God. And Moses, in one place, when he was speaking to the Israelites, said, "The secret things belong unto the Lord our God, but those things which are revealed, belong unto us and to our children."

The doctors in the Temple couldn't tell the boy Jesus every thing. He asked questions and answered questions, and sought to know things; but then, after all, he waited eighteen years to know more, before he began to preach to others and to teach them. And we must all be willing to wait if we would truly learn, for you know we read "he that believeth shall not make haste."

Listen to these lines about waiting:

"A strong and mailéd angel
   With eyes serene and deep,
Unwearied and unwearying
   His patient watch doth keep.

"A strong and mailéd angel,
   In the midnight and the day,
Walking with me at my labor,
   Kneeling with me when I pray.

"Low are the words he speaketh,
   'Young dreamer, God is great;
'Tis glorious to suffer,
   'Tis majesty to wait!'

"O, Angel of endurance!
   O, saintly and sublime!
White are the arméd legions
   That tread the halls of time.

"O, strong and mailéd angel!
Thy trailing robes I see.
Read other souls the lesson
So meekly read to me.

"Still chant the same grand anthem,
The beautiful and great:
'Tis glorious to suffer,
'Tis majesty to wait.'"

"Sitting in the midst of the doctors, both hearing them, and asking them questions."

Here is a great lesson for us all from the boyhood of Jesus.

This story teaches us that we must learn how to think for ourselves. And we must learn how to think in these four ways:

First. We must know how to ask questions.

Second. We must know how to answer them.

Third. We must *try* to know more, and

Fourth. We must *wait* to know more.

And in this way we will be like Jesus Christ when he was a boy. We will increase in wisdom as in stature, and in favor with God and man.

VI.

Samson's Riddle.

SAMSON'S RIDDLE.

"Out of the eater came forth meat, and out of the strong came forth sweetness."—JUDGES xiv. 14.

THESE words were a riddle. You know we all like riddles and conundrums and rebuses.

All your children's papers and magazines have riddles and rebuses in them. Then there are Scripture puzzles and enigmas, for Sunday reading and puzzling; though it seems to me all this is very like the little boy who said, when his mother told him that he must not draw a picture of a horse on his slate on Sunday, that the horse he was drawing was taking the people to church. But to come back to the riddles. People always have had them and always will have them. And one of the most curious things about it all is, that many of these riddles and conundrums which we have nowadays, are as old as the hills. Some have come from the philosophers of Egypt, in the land of the Sphynx and the pyramids, and some have come from King Solomon and the book of Proverbs, and some have descended to us all the way from the wise men of Greece. Solomon, you know, said that there was nothing new under the sun; and I haven't a doubt but that the little boys and girls of ancient Greece and Rome had their own nursery rhymes, very much like those of Mother Goose about "Humpty Dumpty," and "water, water, put out fire: fire, fire, burn stick," and "Eliza, Elizabeth, Betsey and Bess," who "went over the river to find a bird's nest." Why look at this story of ours, where our text is found to day. A war grew out of a riddle, just as in ancient history nations fought over the riddle-like sayings of the Grecian oracles.

This is the story. Samson, the strongest man mentioned in the Bible, fell in love with a Philistine young woman, and he asked his father and mother to go and get her for him. This isn't the way our young men go about getting a wife. In these days, very often, the young men feel themselves perfectly adequate to the occasion, and would never think of letting their parents do all the courting. But Samson's parents said that this young woman would not do. They said she was a Philistine, an enemy of their country, belonging to a nation the Israelites were forever fighting with; and they made up their minds that it wasn't the thing, and would never do at all. But, like a great many other parents, all their objections were in vain, and Samson had his own way and married the Philistine woman.

Now it is very evident that Samson hated the Philistines with all his heart, though, perhaps, he had fallen in love with this girl, who might have captivated him with her pretty face. So he made an incident which happened to him on his way down to Timnath for the first time, an occasion for provoking the Philistine young men who came to the wedding afterwards. On his journey to see his lady-love, as he came near to the vineyards of Timnath, a young lion came out from the thickets and roared against him. Samson thereupon walked right up to the fellow and rent him, just as a man in a drygoods store rips down a piece of muslin, with a great tearing noise. The Bible says he rent him "as he would have rent a kid, and he had nothing in his hand"; but we read, "he told not his father or his mother what he had done." I wonder how many of us would have kept that thing to ourselves. I rather think some of us would have told the first person we met, and would have gone for the nearest policeman, to bring the lion we had killed into the town. And I think we would hunt through the local items in the evening's newspaper, to see if a correct account of the affair had been given. But Samson said nothing about it to any one, and some weeks afterwards, when he was going down to be married and to have his great wedding feast, when he came near to

Samson's Riddle.

the place he turned aside to see what had become of the lion's body. There it was, a rotting carcass; but down in one corner of the bones he saw some bees, and a honeycomb which they had built there. Then he took a lot of the honey in his hand, and ate some of it himself and gave the rest to his father and mother. Then they had the wedding and the great wedding feast, which lasted seven days, a long time for a party.

Now just see how a riddle broke up a pleasant party, and separated Samson from his newly married wife, and brought on a war between two countries.

There were thirty persons present at this feast, as Samson's companions. I suppose these people were all Philistines, probably young men and women. Well, when the feast had begun, what does Samson, who was always a great mischief-maker, do, but begin to bother his guests with a conundrum or a riddle. You know when a conundrum is started, people like to answer it. They don't like to appear stupid and feel compelled to say, "I give it up." It isn't pleasant to be considered dull. We all like to guess things right off, and be counted bright. This was what troubled these Philistines at Samson's party. They couldn't guess his riddle, they weren't smart enough; and Samson, no doubt, let them see that he enjoyed catching them. I am sorry to say that Samson, though an Israelite, set them an example of betting. He said, "If ye can certainly declare it unto me within the seven days of the feast, and find it out, then I will give you thirty sheets and thirty change of garments: but if ye can not declare it me, then shall ye give me thirty sheets and thirty change of garments." This was a good haul Samson made on them, for his housekeeping purposes in his married life; and as he felt he had them, it began to make the Philistines as mad as hornets. This was the riddle: "Out of the eater came forth meat, and out of the strong came forth sweetness." Well; they tried to find out this answer for three days, but all in vain. I suppose all this time Samson kept nag-

Samson's Riddle.   161

ging at them, and worrying them and teasing them, to know if they had found out his riddle, telling them that he was pretty sure to get the linen and the clothes, until the Philistines told Samson's wife that if she did not find out the riddle for them they would burn her up, and would burn down her father's house with fire. They said: "Have ye called us to take that we have," or "to impoverish us?" You see they didn't want to pay this wager, and then they were jealous of Samson. So the poor wife of Samson cried and took on for seven days, and had after all a very sad honeymoon of it. She begged Samson to tell her the answer to the riddle; but he replied that he hadn't even told his mother and father, and he didn't mean to tell his wife. But she begged so hard that at last he told her, and she went right straight off to her friends saying, "I've got it! I've found it out!"

So it came to pass that before the sun went down on the seventh day the men spoke up and said:

"We've guessed it, we've found it out! What is sweeter than honey, and what is stronger than a lion!"

"Yes," said Samson. "I know how you've found it out; my wife has told you; for if ye had not ploughed with my heifer ye had not found out my riddle!"

Then it was Samson's turn to get angry, and he went down to Ashkelon, a rich Philistine city, and deliberately killed thirty citizens there, like any highway robber, and took their sheets and garments, and gave them to the thirty guests at his table. Then he was done with his new friends and his new wife, and leaving them all at Timnath, he went back with his father and mother, and lived in their house like a great spoiled boy; and the man who had been Samson's groomsman, or "best man," married Samson's deserted wife.

Now, my dear children, did you ever hear of such a story as this? Did you ever hear the like? Would you believe such a thing could ever happen, and happen in the Bible, among the Israelites, God's own chosen people?

A man goes down to a foreign city, and kills a lion and eats honey out of his dead body days afterwards; gets married; gives a great feast; proposes a riddle; offers a bet; makes the whole company angry; gets angry himself; is given away by his wife; kills thirty men to pay his wager; leaves his wife and packs his trunk and goes back again to live at his father's house;—just as if nothing had ever happened! This was indeed the dark ages in the history of the Israelites. Every man did that which was right in his own eyes. There was no king, and there were no good prophets, and the good judges were dead.

Samson lived about 1,140 years before Christ; over a hundred years before the days of Samuel and Saul and David. He was a great mischief-maker: a sort of hazing sophomore, looking out all the time for jokes to be played on people; and he was so full-blooded and careless about human life, that he thought no more of killing sixty or a hundred men than of shooting so many snipe or rabbits.

But then this great, untamed giant, sniffing the blood of the Philistines wherever he went, was at last caught by them. They put his eyes out, and took away his strength, and finally made him their slave grinding in a mill, while they derided him. We all know how he died. His former strength was given back to him, and he died by bowing down the pillars of the Temple where the Philistines had met together to make sport of him; and 3,000 Philistines died with him in this his last act of destruction.

The great musical composer, Handel, has written an oratorio about Samson; and you can hear in the last music of that piece, the crush of the building and the noise of the final catastrophe. John Milton, too, the pure English poet, has described Samson crying out in his blindness, in the poem called "Samson Agonistes," or Samson the Struggler.

SAMSON'S RIDDLE.   165

"O dark, dark, dark amid the blaze of noon,
Irrecoverably dark; total eclipse
Without all hope of day!
Oh first created beam and these great words,
'Let there be light,' and light was over all.
Why am I thus bereaved thy prime decree?
The sun to me is dark,
And silent as the moon
When she deserts the night,
Hid in her vacant interlunar cave."

Our text to-day, then, is a riddle, and all riddles and conundrums and proverbs are based upon some truth, or upon some catch or perverted bit of truth. When the New England Hospital for Women and Children had a fair three years ago, there was published a book full of conundrums, which was sold for the benefit of the hospital. I never saw so many conundrums together, and one feels tired enough after he has tried to guess the three hundred and thirtieth conundrum in that book. Then there are so many riddles in the world which puzzle our brains to try and find them out. There is a long one, in poetry, of nearly a hundred lines, and the answer is found in a certain verse in one of the books of the Old Testament.

It begins in this way:

"Come and commiserate
One who is blind,
Hopeless and desolate,
Void of a mind,
Guileless and deceiving.
Though unbelieving,
Free from all sin.

"By mortal adored,
Still I ignored
The world I was in.
King Ptolemy's, Cæsar's,
Tiglote's, Pilesar's
Birthdays are known—
Wise men, astrologers,
All are acknowledgers—
Mine is unknown.

"I ne'er had a father,
Or mother, or brother.
If I had either,
Then they were neither
Alive at my birth.
Lodged in a palace,

Samson's Riddle.

Hunted by malice,
I did not inherit,
By lineage or merit,
A spot in the earth.
Compassed by dangers,
Nothing could harm me;
By foemen and strangers,
Naught could alarm me.
I saved, I destroyed,
I blessed, I annoyed,
Kept a crown for a prince,
But had none of my own;
Filled the place of a king,
But ne'er had a throne.
Rescued a warrior,
Baffled a plot,
Was what I seemed not,
Seemed what I was not.
Devoted to slaughter,
A price on my head,
A king's lovely daughter
Watched by my bed.
Though gently she nursed me,
Fainting with fear,
She never caressed me
Nor wiped off a tear."

And then, after a number of verses, it ends in this way:

"I lived not, I died not,
Yet tell you, I must,
That ages have passed
Since I turned into dust.

"This paradox whence?
This squalor, this splendor?
Say, am I a king?
Or a silly pretender?
Fathom this mystery
Deep in my history.
Am I a man?
An angel supernal?
A demon infernal?
Solve it who can."

Do any of you know the answer to this riddle? What is it? If you want to know, look at I Samuel, 19th chapter, 13th and following verses. Isn't that a wonderful riddle?

There is truth, then, under these riddles, though the truth is hidden from us, and puts on a false face, like those false faces we buy in the stores, and put on to frighten one another with. It's very hard to realize that there is a living face behind the false face.

SAMSON'S RIDDLE. 169

And that is what makes it so hard to find out the true answer to these riddles. But there is truth to them all! Look, for instance, at some of our well-known proverbs. "Birds of a feather flock together." This means that people who like each other, because they are alike will keep together. "There's as good fish in the sea as ever was caught." This means that there are other places and other people beside the set that we go with. "A stitch in time saves nine," "A bird in the hand is worth two in the bush," "Make hay while the sun shines," are all proverbs which have a clear and simple meaning; and we know how many more there are of the same sort, when we sit down to play proverbs.

But now what does Samson's riddle mean: "Out of the eater came forth meat, and out of the strong came forth sweetness?"

I suppose the thirty young Philistines who were Samson's guests at the wedding feast at Timnath, puzzled their heads over this thing, and kept saying to themselves, "Out of the eater—out of the eater. What does that mean? Came forth meat. How could meat come out of an eater? What does the man mean? And out of the strong—the strong what? What is the strong? And out of the strong came forth sweetness. What does that mean? Who can guess it?"

And I suppose they kept nudging each other and saying to themselves, when they came to the table, "Say, have you found it out yet?" And then, no doubt, one would raise his eyebrows at another across the table, and the man who was asked in this way, would frown back and nod his head, as much as to say, "No, sir; don't ask me!"

Well, my dear children, I don't want to tease you any longer, as Samson teased his guests at the wedding, and so I will tell you plainly what I think this riddle means, and what it teaches us. Of course, to Samson it only meant a dead lion with a swarm of bees in it; but he put this fact in such a way, by the words of his riddle, that the dead lion and the living bees become a sort of proverb, with a deeper meaning to it.

SAMSON'S RIDDLE. 171

I think, then, this riddle teaches us two truths. They are these:
Destroyers can become sustainers, and
Strength can be turned into sweetness.

I.

First of all, I said, Destroyers can become sustainers.

Now this sounds very heavy, I know. It reads like some of the books on political economy, or the science of civilization. But we can soon crack it up into little bits of truth, as we do when we tap a big piece of soft coal on the hearth, with the poker, and it crackles into little bits and burns. Some time ago a German scholar, who was very poor (not a very *poor scholar*), said to me when he was explaining, in broken English, his poverty, "Ah me! I am verra poor; I have one wife and six leetle boys to support, and zay all hang on to me. Zay are all consumers; not one of zem is a producer." What the poor man meant by this was, that they all depended upon him to make a living for them; none of them did any thing for themselves. They were all consumers, or destroyers of food; none of them were producers, or sustainers.

I tell you, my dear children, it's a great thing to be able to become sustainers and help along, instead of all the time living off of other people. St. Paul told his converts that he was unwilling to become burdensome to any of them, and so he worked at tent-making when he was short of money, instead of going about with a long face and a subscription paper, saying that they hadn't paid him his salary, and that if his travelling expenses were not paid he wouldn't go to Corinth or Ephesus any more. This being a minister only to be supported, or merely for the sake of getting a living, is the poorest work in the world. It won't stand in the day of trial. Our Saviour said that the "hireling fleeth, because he is an hireling."

There is a time in our lives, then, and it comes to some of us earlier than to others, when we ought to change from being mere destroyers, or consumers, into sustainers and producers. "Out of the eater" there ought to "come forth meat." I know to-day a very celebrated doctor of divinity who, when he was a young man studying for the ministry, taught in a night-school, so that he might help his father, who was a country clergyman, to educate the younger children. I knew and loved a dear fellow-student for the ministry, who wrote for magazines and took some pupils, on purpose to educate at college the son of a man who never could have sent his boy to college. And I have known young ladies who, instead of crying over lost fortunes and changes in their family affairs, have turned to, like brave girls, and have taught music and drawing, and copied lawyers' documents, so that all the load might not come upon their poor broken-spirited parents.

God be praised, my dear children, for all this brave and busy strength of character, which can turn deadness into activity, and can make a swarm of busy bees, each with his own little store of food, come out of and take the place of some once strong lion who has been killed by a passing business freak, or some Samson-like mischief-maker.

What you boys and girls must remember above every thing else is, that you must *never be ashamed to work*, that you must never be ashamed of any thing in this world but sin, that you mustn't always hang upon your parents and depend upon them, but that you ought to be ready and willing to do whatever you can yourself to be helpful to those at home, so that you may be like the busy bees, who made honey; and not like the lion, who is a great eater, or consumer, and goes about all the time looking after food.

And then this first lesson has another side to it. We do love to destroy things. Some people have what the phrenologists, who examine heads, call the "bump of destructiveness." Some people break chairs and china and glass tumblers, and use up their clothes fearfully; while other people are very careful, and never think of breaking things.

"He's dreadful hard on his clothes, sir," is what a poor woman once said to me when I was asking her if she didn't think she was coming too often to me for shoes. "Why," she went on, "John can't set wunst into his Sunday clothes for a whole day without their being all wriggled up and mussed, while Ann Eliza, over there, always looks as if she had come right out of the bandbox!"

Now there is no use of denying the fact, my dear children, that we have got this love of destroying things, this destructiveness, as it is called, within us, and we must try and overcome it. Some children like to break their toys and tear their books, and pick flowers apart and kill insects. I believe this destructiveness comes, after all we may say about it, from the devil. He is called, in the Revelation of St. John, Apollyon the destroyer. I remember a book once that tried to prove that Napoleon's name was taken from Apollyon, because he was such a great destroyer. It is God-like to create and to build up; it is devil-like to destroy. It is easy enough to go about burning houses and tearing up flowers and killing animals; but how hard it is to create that which we have destroyed.

Think of the French Revolution; think of the Commune in Paris eight years ago. Palaces were destroyed, citizens were shot, money was wasted, whole streets were burned down by blazing petroleum cars, and all for nothing. Paris was like a city full of lions, which were destroyers, going about to devour whatever they could find. Alexander the Great, Hannibal, Attila the Scourge of God, as he was called, Tamerlane, Napoleon, Frederick, Charles XII., were great destroyers.

One time in the history of our Lord when he was upon earth, James and John wanted to bring down fire upon a certain Samaritan village, because they did not seem disposed to welcome them; but Jesus rebuked them and called them Boanerges, "the sons of thunder," and said that he came not to destroy but to fulfil; and that his meat was to do the will of him that sent him.

But even our natural love of destruction can be changed into a love of creation. Look at St. Paul. He wanted to destroy the Christian Church, but God changed his nature, and killed the old lion in him, and "out of the eater there came forth meat."

II.

There is one other lesson this riddle teaches us. It is this: *Strength can be turned into sweetness.*

This lion, which had only lived to eat other animals, and to destroy life wherever he could find it, became, when he was dead, the home for some little insects, which went about finding sweets among the flowers and bringing them home to the hive. The lion's strength was gone, and in the place of it there was the bee's sweetness.

It isn't very often, my dear children, that we see strength and sweetness combined.

You see it sometimes among trained animals, such as dogs and horses. I have seen a little bit of a boy riding a great big horse—and the horse was just as gentle as a kitten. But when we have power and are very strong, we are apt to be rough and harsh. And it has been because certain people in the Christian Church have forgotten about the gentleness of Jesus, and have only thought of him as the Judge of the world, that they have exalted the Virgin Mary with power, and have prayed to her in her sweetness and gentleness to intercede with her divine Son on their behalf.

David says, in one place, speaking of God, "Thy gentleness hath made me great." Think of the gentleness of God, who is omnipotent.

When the English king, Edward III., captured the city of Calais in France, he was so angry with the citizens for holding out so long, that he threatened to burn the city and kill the inhabitants.

Thereupon six of the principal citizens, the

THE BURGHERS OF CALAIS AND KING EDWARD III.
W. Gate. p. 178

burgomasters, or aldermen, went before the king with halters around their necks, begging him to hang them, but to spare the city. The king was for taking them at their word, and would have had them dangling in a few minutes from the nearest tree, but Edward's wife, Philippa, the queen, interceded for them and begged them off.

And in very much the same way we all need to have around us gentle, kind influences, to make us sweet and tender, and to keep our strength, or even our healthfulness, from becoming harsh and rough. Every man is the better for a true, pure wife's influence over him, and the boys of a family will never know until they have grown up, and are alone and away from home, how very much they have been benefited by the influence of their little sisters upon them.

"Out of the eater came forth meat, and out of the strong came forth sweetness."

Destroyers can become sustainers, and strength can be turned into sweetness.

These are the two lessons we learn from Samson's riddle.

Pray to God, my dear children, through Jesus Christ, that you may become of use in the world, and that you may be tender as well as strong, for sweetness without strength is weak, and strength without sweetness is incomplete; but sweetness *and* strength is what God wants in the life and character of all his children.

Jesus was called the Lion of the tribe of Judah, and yet he is the Lamb of God, who came to take away the sins of the world.

VII.

Running Aground.

RUNNING AGROUND.

"And falling into a place where two seas met, they ran the ship aground."—ACTS xxvii. 41.

WERE you ever on board a ship that ran aground? If you never were, let me tell you how it feels. Once on the Mississippi River, once on the North River, and once in Martha's Vineyard, I have been on board a boat which has got upon some bar and has stuck fast there. Each time that I have got aground it has been in the night, and it has taken until noon the next day for the steamboat to get off the mud-bank, and to go upon her way again. One night when I was coming down from Albany to New York, all of a sudden the machinery stopped. Then I felt the bottom of the boat scraping on the bed of the river, just as a row-boat scrapes upon the sand, when it lands upon the beach. It was a foggy night, but when we were up on deck we could see five or six other steamers which were in the same predicament. They were blowing off steam, and were tugging and straining to get away from the sand-bar. If you have ever seen a dozen flies stuck in molasses, or upon the "catch-em-alive-o," sticky paper, you have seen a picture of ships that have run aground.

Now there is only one of two things to do when a ship has run aground:

First. We can throw the cargo overboard. This will lighten the boat and let her float off; but then, think what an awful waste it is to destroy a whole cargo. Or,

Second. We can wait for a rise of the tide, in hopes that when it comes it will float our vessel. But, perhaps, even this will not lift us far enough.

So that you see, in any case, it is a bad thing to run aground.

Now in this story where our text is found,

we have given to us a full description of St. Paul's shipwreck at sea.

He was being carried as a prisoner to Rome, having appealed to the Emperor Nero for protection from the decision of Felix and Festus; just as in these days a man may appeal from the decision of a judge in any court, and may carry the matter up to the Supreme Court.

There were soldiers to keep him, and a centurion or captain to direct the Roman soldiers, and altogether there was a large party on board. If you will read the twenty-seventh chapter of the Acts of the Apostles, you will see for yourselves what a long and tempestuous voyage they had, and how many adventures they met with, on their long and stormy journey to Rome.

St. Paul told the captain of the vessel, beforehand, that they would have a long and stormy voyage, and that they had better not set sail from Crete. But the captain thought that St. Paul was only a poor landsman who knew nothing about sailing, and only a Roman prisoner, whose opinion was not worth consulting, and so he set out on the voyage.

Then they ran into a furious gale, and were tossed up and down the Mediterranean. It is interesting to notice what they did in this heavy blow. It lasted over fourteen days, and at last they gave up all hope of their lives. They put ropes and chains under the vessel to keep her from going to pieces, and they cast four anchors out of the stern, but it was all of no use. The great, heavy, lumbering grain vessel was filled with water and seemed to be settling down, and the sailors began to get into the life-boats to save themselves, when St. Paul said to the captain, or centurion, "Except these abide in the ship, ye can not be saved." This was a selfish, cowardly sort of thing for the sailors to do—this making for the boats—to save their own lives. I remember one time when I was on this same Mediterranean Sea, coming up from Naples to Genoa, that we were in a heavy fog, and were run into by a large vessel, and were cut down to the water's

Running Aground.

edge. The vessel was filled with Italian soldiers. It was a terribly dark and stormy night, and we were all upon deck, wondering what would come next, when all of a sudden the Italian soldiers seized the boats and began to go off in them. If the vessel had gone down we would all have been drowned like rats in a cage, for we had no means of escape left us. Well, just in this same way, the sailors on this vessel where St. Paul was, seized the boats, and were making off and were leaving the ships, when the apostle stopped them, and told the captain that he must save the boats and not let the sailors go.

At last, after they had listened to St. Paul's cheering words of hope, and had heeded his advice, and had partaken of some food, they threw out their cargo of wheat, and hoisted the mainsail, and let go the rudder-bands, and made for the shore, to beach the boat, and then strike out for the land. And then the words of our text occur: "And falling into a place where two seas met, they ran the ship aground; and the fore part stuck fast and remained unmovable, but the hinder part was broken with the violence of the waves." Then some of the soldiers,—what mean, selfish fellows they were,—proposed that they should kill Paul and the other prisoners, for fear they would escape when they got to land, and would run away as fast as their legs could carry them. But the centurion who had charge of the prisoners and the soldiers wanted to save Paul, so he gave command that they who could swim should go first to lead the way, and that the others should follow after as well as they could. So the brave ones who could swim struck out first for the shore, and the others followed: "Some on boards, and some on broken pieces of the ship. And so it came to pass that they escaped all safe to land."

This is the story of St. Paul's shipwreck as given so graphically in the twenty-seventh chapter of the book of the Acts of the Apostles. Read it for yourselves, in your own Bibles, and you will see how wonderfully it is there described. We can see it all for ourselves! There is the old stranded ship, with the surf breaking over her; there are the swimmers making their way through the waves; there are the rest of the party clinging on to masts and spars of the vessel, and all landing safe and sound on the beach; and, last of all, we see the barbarous people of the island on which they had struck, the island of Melita, coming down to the help of the poor, shipwrecked party, and helping them to make a fire on the beach to warm themselves and dry their wet clothes.

We can see Paul hurrying about to get a bundle of sticks to make a fire with, and shaking off the snake which came out of the sticks into the fire; and away off on the sand-bar we can see the old ship knocked by the waves and going to pieces, on that spot on which she had run aground, where the two seas met; just as the steamer Huron went ashore the other night in the gale, down on the North Carolina shore by Kitty Hawk.

"*Running aground.*" This is our subject to-day.

Now it's a bad thing to run aground with a vessel! It's a sad sight to see some grand vessel stranded on the rocks, or on the beach, and going to pieces there when all the time she ought to be sailing free over the ocean.

But, my dear children, I'll tell you what is a sadder sight than to see a ship aground. It is to see a human soul stranded and powerless; it is to see a nature which ought to be sailing along over the Sea of Time to Heaven, stuck fast in the things of this world; in some bad habit, or course of life, which holds the soul fast, so that it is like a ship aground, and can not move forward.

Here we are, then, trying to make our way through this world, just as a ship beats out of a harbor, and sails on the ocean, and enters another harbor. There are rocks and bars and sand-banks and breakers around us at every turn. There are evil habits in our soul, and our natures are weak and sinful, just like a leaky ship, and there are great and terrible temptations around us all.

St. Paul says, in one place, that we must through much tribulation enter into the kingdom of heaven. It seems as if this stormy voyage of St. Paul on the Mediterranean Sea, was in some respects very much like our voyage of life. We don't know what is before us in life; we don't know what storms are to break upon us; we don't know what our voyage is to be like. What, then, shall we do, to keep ourselves from running aground, and sticking fast and breaking in pieces?

We must do these four things:

I.

First of all, if we would avoid running aground, *we must keep a steady course.*

How often, on board a steamer that is going out to sea, down the intricate channel of some harbor, we hear that word of command given by the pilot on the wheel-house — "*steady.*" St. James says, in his epistle, that if we would receive the reward of our prayers we must ask with a steady faith, "nothing wavering; for he that wavereth is like a wave of the sea driven with the wind and tossed." In other words, if we want to keep on the direct way towards God and heaven, we must be willing and ready to steer a steady course, not turning to the right hand or to the left.

The pilot of a vessel, you know, can not go by any course he pleases; he must steer by his chart and must keep in the true channel. If he tries any experiments, or disobeys the cautions of his chart and sails on the wrong side of the buoys, he must be prepared to get into trouble by surely running aground.

Many a time I have gone down Boston harbor with the ocean steamers, and have watched the pilot on the wheelhouse, and the helmsmen in the steering-room. The pilot gives the signal, and a bell is rung to the man in the steering-house, and an indicator marks upon a dial plate the words "starboard," "port," "steady." And in this way the great, majestic steamer, minding her helm and the word of the pilot, keeps her course according to the chart and keeps from running aground. But the little fellows,—the sail-boats and sloops and light weights,—run across the harbor; because, since they don't draw much water, they can run pretty much wherever they choose.

Some time ago, down in the Chesapeake Bay, the captain of an oyster shallop was going up the harbor to Norfolk after oysters. When he went down below, he called a colored man he had on board, who was a landsman and didn't know any thing about sailing, to take the helm.

"Now, Jim," said the captain, "do you see that bright star right in front of the foremast?"

"Yes, massah," replied Jim. "You mean dat ar bright fellow in front?"

"Yes," said the captain, "that bright star up there that looks like a cat's eye in the dark. Well, now keep that star right in front of you all the time, steer by that star, and all will go well. Now, then, I'm going down below, and be sure you keep her steady."

"Yes, sah," replied the colored man, "you trust Dandy Jim from North Caroline."

So the captain went down below for the dog-watch and took his nap. Meanwhile Jim got tired of holding on to the tiller, and went forward to look at something shining there, over the bow of the boat, when all of a sudden the boat gave a lunge, and the sails gibed over, and as Jim was trying to get things straight on deck, up came the captain to see how things were going on.

"Halloo, Jim," he cried, "what are you about? Where are you steering her to? Why here's that star I told you to keep right in front of the mainmast, away behind our stern."

"Bless um heart, massah," said Jim, "dat's nothing; we've sailed by him an hour ago."

And very much in this same way, my children, we trifle with the helm, and let go the tiller, for the sake of looking at something shining around us, and forget to keep our

Running Aground. 195

eyes ever looking steadily at the star we are to steer by, until we get out of our course altogether. There are many people who think, with this colored man on the oyster boat in the Chesapeake, that they have sailed far away past the star they ought to steer by, when all the while they have only turned their back upon it, and are sailing in the opposite direction. Some boys, when they grow up, think it is not worth their trouble to keep the star in front of the foremast; they don't read their Bibles, which is like consulting the chart, and they don't look out for the light ahead; and thus their course is a crooked one, something like the way a fly flies, and before they know it they will run the ship aground, and will become stuck fast and remain unmovable.

The ancients used to talk a great deal about sailing between Scylla and Charybdis. These were two great difficulties in the Mediterranean Sea, near Sicily. One was a rock, and the other was a whirlpool, and at times, when the sailors would try to avoid the one danger they would fall into the other; and in this way it has become a proverb, that in avoiding Scylla we may fall into Charybdis.

And then, too, in trying to be Christians, we must keep a steady course, lest we run aground on truths which are only half truths.

There was a ferryman once, away up in Canada, who used to row people over the St. Lawrence River at a certain place. He was an old hunter and trapper, and when the English missionaries came out there he became a Christian. Sometimes he used to have long arguments and talks with the people he carried over. There was one old hunter up there who, when he became a Christian, was very much troubled about the doctrine of faith and works. He didn't know which he ought to use, faith or works. Martin, the ferryman, used to hear his old companion talking in this way as he rowed him over the river, and he thought he would teach him a lesson. So he had his two oars painted, one with the word "faith," and the other with the word "works." Then the next time his friend came to be carried over the ferry, when he got well out on the stream, he dropped one oar and pulled on the other.

"What are you doing?" asked the trapper.

"I'm holding on to works alone," replied Martin

"Pull on the other oar," cried the trapper, "we're only going round and round. We're not going forward one bit."

So Martin dropped the oar marked "*works*," and pulled on the oar marked "faith."

"Hold on," cried the trapper, "now you're wrong, too. See, you're going round and round in the opposite direction. Pull with both oars."

"Well, now," replied Martin, "*do you the same;* have faith and use works, and go straight forward; don't go round and round with one oar only."

Thus it is with us, my dear children. We must keep a steady course if we would keep from running aground. We must pull straight forward. This is our first lesson.

II.

Secondly: If we would keep from running aground we must know our soundings. When that splendid steamer of the White Star Line, the Atlantic, went ashore on the coast of Nova Scotia a few years ago, it was all because the captain didn't know where he was; he didn't take enough soundings; the lead wasn't dropped every few minutes; he thought he was further out at sea than he really was, and there that splendid steamer, with all on board, went bang up upon the rocks, with a full head of steam on, just as if she was well out at sea.

My dear children, we must learn to know just where we are; just how far, or how near, we are to the rocks and headlands of danger. We must know ourselves; we must know our own hearts; we must sound ourselves, examine ourselves, and look into our own souls, to find out where we stand. "If we say that we have no sin, we deceive ourselves, and the truth is not in us." We are on dangerous ground without knowing it. How often we read in fairy stories of enchanted ground, where nothing could hurt people; and of dangerous ground, where they were in great need of being careful, for fear they might be caught by evil ones. Dangerous ground! Oh, my dear children, there is a great deal of this in the world; it is around us at every turn. We are like sailors trying to beat up an intricate harbor. We must know the chart, and mind the pilot, and keep inside of the buoys; and we must throw the lead overboard and sound often, to know where we really are.

George Herbert, the dear old English poet, says in one of his poems, in his quaint way:

"By all means use sometime to be alone;
  Salute thyself; see what thy soul dost wear:
  Dare to look in thy chest—for 'tis thine own—
  And tumble up and down what thou findest there."

He calls our soul a trunk, a chest, like a sailor's chest; and he tells us to open it and look into it, and not to be afraid to tumble our thoughts and feelings up and down there.

Yes, my dear children, we must know *ourselves;* we must learn to look into our souls; we must throw the line down, and find out how we stand and what we are doing. We *must* know where we are, if we would keep from running aground. Some time ago, on the coast of Norway, an English barque was in a heavy fog. The captain didn't know where he was; he couldn't get a glimpse of the sun; he couldn't take an observation, and altogether the vessel was on dangerous ground.

"Isn't it well mother don't know where we are?" said the captain's little boy to him one morning at breakfast.

"Yes, my son, it is," replied the father; "but it would be much better for all hands on board if we only knew where we were ourselves."

My dear children, do you know just where you are? Do you think you see your hearts as God sees them? Do you know what your temptations are? Do you know what your evil habits are? Or are you all in a fog?

If you want to keep from running aground and being dashed to pieces, you must know where you are; you must take your soundings.

III.

Thirdly: If we would avoid running aground, we must beware of cross-currents. It was these opposite tides which did the work for St. Paul's ship. One current took hold of the bow, and another took hold of the stern, and swung them around in opposite ways, and thus the ship was broken in pieces by these warring currents. Now we must be very careful in life about these opposite currents. For instance, here is a boy who wants to be a Christian and honor his father and mother, and yet he likes to go with certain boys whose influence over him isn't good, simply for the sake of the fun those boys have. He wants to do right, and yet he wants to have a good time with those boys he knows his mother and father don't like him to go with! He is like the ship in the place where two seas meet.

Now we all meet these cross-currents in life; and oh, how hard it is to keep out of them! We want to study our lessons, and yet we want to play; we want to serve Jesus Christ, and yet we want to please ourselves; we want to keep from sin, and yet we like certain people who don't think it is wrong to do what we wouldn't dare to do; and it's a very hard matter to keep clear of these currents and eddies, which swing us around out of our course.

Dear children, I remember what it was, when a boy, to feel these currents running by me very rapidly; and oh, I know what it is now to feel their influence! It is like the dangerous undertow which we feel sometimes when we bathe in the surf. But we must keep out of their way, or we will be like St. Paul in his voyage, and "falling into a place where two seas met," we will run our souls aground.

You know there is a saying about "Riding two horses, and coming to the ground between them." It's a hard thing to ride two horses; to have a foot on each of them, and yet to be able to keep on at all. And it's very hard to keep our course straight and steady, if all the while we are tossed, first by one tide and then by the opposite one, and have our wills swung around all the while, first by one current and then wrenched about by another. *Steady's the word.* Beware of these cross-currents.

IV.

And then *lastly:* If we would keep from running aground, we must trust our pilot. When the pilot comes on board a vessel he takes full command, and the captain has nothing whatever to say. Then the crew must mind not the old commander, but the new one. The man on the lookout and the man at the wheel must each obey the commands of the pilot. He has charge of the vessel now, and he alone will be answerable for her. And there must not be any disobedience on board. Every one must agree with the pilot. Some time ago a schooner was sailing along Long Island Sound. The captain and the mate didn't get on well together. At last, when the mate suggested to the captain that he should steer the boat in a certain direction, the captain got very angry and, swearing at the mate, said:

"You go down and take care of your end of the vessel and I'll take care of mine."

"All right," said the mate, and he went to the bow of the boat. Presently a splash was heard in the water, and the mate sang out: "Halloo, captain! my end of the boat is anchored. How is your end coming on?"

Now we can't get on in this way, if we're trying to serve our Lord Jesus Christ. We mustn't try to manage our end of the boat. We must put our faith in our Pilot, and do what he bids us. When he comes into our souls we must give up the command to him. The old captain oughtn't to rule any longer.

Some time ago I was visiting a physician, who was ill. He was waiting for the doctor to come.

"Why, doctor," said I, "you're a physician yourself. Why don't you treat yourself without calling in another?"

"Ah," said he, "I'm sick now; I can't trust myself. I want to give myself up to another; I have no faith in my own skill now, I'm so weak. This sickness has taken away all my trust in myself."

And that was the only thing for the poor sick doctor to do.

And, children, it's the only thing that we can do. You and I must give ourselves up to Jesus Christ our Saviour, and we must ask him to take charge of us. Yes, day and night we must pray for his help: when we're tired, when we're tempted, when we're naughty, when every thing seems to go wrong, all we can do is to pray to Christ to come and take charge of our souls, just as the pilot comes on board the vessel and keeps it from running aground. Listen to this verse of a beautiful hymn to Christ, which the English poet Palgrave wrote for little children:

> "Be beside me in the night,
> Close by me till morning light;
> Make me gentle, kind, and true,
> Do what mother bids me do;
> Help and cheer me when I fret,
> And forgive when I forget."

And now, in closing, let me say: Remember these lessons.

If we would keep from running aground on the snares and temptations of this life, we must do these four things:

We must keep a steady course; we must know where we are; we must avoid crosscurrents; and we must obey our Pilot.

And if we do these things we will be brought at last to that haven where we would be, safe and sound, and not on boards and broken pieces of the ship, as St. Paul's companions did when they were shipwrecked and the vessel was run aground.

VIII.

Carriages to Jerusalem.

CARRIAGES TO JERUSALEM.

"And after those days we took up our carriages, and went up to Jerusalem."—Acts xxi. 15.

CARRIAGES to Jerusalem! This sounds strangely. It reads as if the apostles were on a journey in those days, and having arrived at a depot or railway station, found some carriages awaiting them there, and took up their line of travel, and went on the rest of the way to their journey's end. It is very difficult for us to take these words literally. How could the apostles take up their carriages; and what were their carriages to Jerusalem?

Now the difficulty disappears when we remember that the word carriage, in the Bible, means baggage, packages, bundles; or, as the English call it, "luggage." In the old Saxon, "luggage" was a word which meant something that had to be lugged or carried about. The word "lug" was from the Anglo-Saxon "geluggian," to drag by the hair, or to haul and tug at something very heavy. In the same way the word "carry" was derived from the old Saxon word "cyren," to turn or bear away; and the word "carriage" meant, originally, the act of carrying or transportation, then the means of conveyance, and last of all, that which is carried. "Carriage" also means one's behavior, or deportment,— the way a person acts or carries himself,— and sometimes it means the management or carrying on of a business.

But in the Bible the word always means the bundles, packages, or load that one has to carry. Here are some of the places where we find the word used with reference to carrying bundles or burdens. "So they turned and departed, and put the little ones and the cattle and the carriage (or baggage) before them" (Judges xviii. 21). This was when the Danites robbed Micah, in the rough days of the judges. Then in the story of David's conflict with Goliath we read, that when he arrived at the camp of the soldiers of Saul, where his brothers were, he "left his carriage in the hands of the keeper of the carriage, and ran into the army and came and saluted his brethren" (1 Sam. xvii. 22). The prophet Isaiah, too, uses this same word to mean baggage, when he says, in speaking of the Assyrian invasion, "at Michmash he hath laid up his carriages" (Isa. x. 28). And again, when this same prophet Isaiah is showing that the idols of Babylon could not save the nation, while God saved his people, he begins that wonderful forty-sixth chapter with these words: "Bel boweth down; Nebo stoopeth; their idols were upon their beasts, and upon their cattle: your carriages were heavy laden; they are a burden to the weary beast."

So then, when St. Luke says in this fifteenth verse of the twenty-first chapter of the Acts, "We took up our carriages, and went up to Jerusalem," it doesn't mean that the apostles got into soft, easy-cushioned carriages, like our cabs and barouches of to-day, and were driven up along the turnpike from Cæsarea to Jerusalem. It means just the opposite of this. It means that, instead of being carried over the difficulties in their way, they took up their difficulties, one by one, in their own hands, and went on their way towards Jerusalem.

The carriages didn't take the apostles up; it was the apostles who stopped and took up their carriages: that is, their bundles, packages, and loads.

This was the way it came about. St. Paul was on his way back to Jerusalem after one of his long missionary expeditions. He wanted to be there in time for the Feast of Pentecost, but he couldn't help stopping over on the journey, to see the different churches which he had planted. When he was at Miletus he sent up to Ephesus for the elders of the church to come and see him. You will read about this in the last part of the twentieth chapter of the book of Acts. It is a very touching scene. After giving them a farewell message, he kneeled down with them on the beach, and prayed with them all. Then, we read, "They all wept sore, and fell on Paul's neck and kissed him, sorrowing most of all for the words which he spake, that they should see his face no more." After this the vessel set sail, and after stopping at the different islands along the coast, the party arrived at Cæsarea, and stayed at the house of Philip the Evangelist. Here they met a prophet named Agabus, who told St. Paul of a very unpleasant time ahead. "He took Paul's girdle and bound his own hands and feet, and said, Thus saith the Holy Ghost, so shall the Jews at Jerusalem bind the man that owneth this girdle, and shall deliver him into the hands of the Gentiles." Then they all begged St. Paul not to go up to Jerusalem, since this man Agabus had prophesied that there was going to be trouble and persecution there.

But they couldn't frighten St. Paul away from his path of duty. He was not afraid of the lions in the way. He turned upon them and said, "What mean ye to weep and to break mine heart? For I am ready not to be bound only, but also to die at Jerusalem for the name of the Lord Jesus." So when they found that they could not turn the apostle from his resolution, they ceased, "saying, The will of the Lord be done." And then the words of our text appear, showing how St. Paul carried his point, and went straight on his way through the trouble that was in store for him. Instead of being carried out of his way, to avoid his duty and the danger that was in it, he took up his burdens and went straight ahead. "After those days," says St. Luke, "we took up our carriages, and went up to Jerusalem." The rest of the story came to pass according to the prophecy of the prophet Agabus.

There was a terrible riot in Jerusalem, made by the Jews on account of St. Paul's preaching, and he was seized by the soldiers and carried off to the castle of Antonius, and afterwards was sent down to Cæsarea under a military escort, to be brought before the Roman governor Felix.

This, then, is the story of our text. Now let us come back to our subject, which is about—

Carrying our own bundles.

I.

Well, then, the first thing we learn from this subject is this: We have all got bundles to carry.

You know how it is in travelling. There are bundles and bags and packages which people take with them in their hands. There are a great many things which are hard to pack up in trunks. High hats, and ladies' bonnets, and umbrellas, and canary-birds in their cages, and babies, can not be packed up. We have to carry these in our hands.

In England gentlemen have hat-boxes and ladies have bandboxes; but here, in this country, men generally wear their hats and ladies their bonnets, so that these articles are carried by being worn.

How many things there are for us to carry

in this world! First, when we are very little children, we carry our toys about with us wherever we go, and take them to bed with us when we go to sleep. Then, when we go to school we carry our books in straps and satchels, and the more books we can put together to carry to school, the bigger we think we are. Then, when we go to college, we carry one or two neat little Latin and Greek books in our hands; and when we grow up, we carry things home to the family; and I think he is a pretty poor kind of man who is ashamed to be seen with a bundle; who is afraid to take up his carriage, or package, for the children or the family, and go on his way towards his Jerusalem-like home.

Then think how much there is for a ship to carry, or for an army to carry with it on its march. The word "impediment" comes from the Latin "*impedimenta*," or the baggage which an army used to have in the old Roman days. There used to be so much to carry that the baggage was the great hindrance, or impediment, to the march. Then, too, if you have ever moved often from house to house, or from city to city, as we ministers do, you will learn that three moves are equal to one fire; for the amount of things which are lost, mislaid, or broken, are almost the same as if the house had been burnt. But besides all these packages and bundles which we have to carry in our every-day life, we have duties and responsibilities to take up, which are just like bundles—big and little—which must be carried. When the old patriot Jacob was dying and blessing his sons, he said of one of them, "Issachar is a strong ass, crouching down between two burdens: and he bowed his shoulder to bear, and became a servant unto tribute." In the Eastern countries they load their camels and horses with bags and boxes and bundles, just as here men load up a dray, or an express wagon. And this son, Issachar, Jacob said, was to be loaded down with burdens and cares and responsibilities.

It does seem as if in this world some people had more than their share of bundles and duties to carry. Some people dodge their duties, and won't carry their own bundles, and are unlike St. Paul's company, who took up their packages and went up to Jerusalem. And then there are others who have very much to carry which don't belong to them. It is just like the wheelers and the leaders in a stage. Perhaps the "off leader" and the "near wheeler," as the driver calls them, have some sort of an understanding between themselves,—at least so it has often seemed to me,—by which the other poor horses do all the pulling, and the heaviest part of the work up-hill and on a level.

Dear children, don't dodge your share of work. Don't let the other horses do all the pulling. Take up your share of the bundles, and the duties; and remember this first lesson of our subject, that in this world we have all got bundles to carry.

II.

The second lesson of our subject is this: Every man must carry his own burden.

In St. Paul's epistle to the Galatians he says, "Bear ye one another's burdens, and thus fulfil the law of Christ." And then a few verses further on he says, "For every man shall bear his own burden." This means that we ought to try to help others who need our help, because, after all, when we have done our utmost to help them, every man will have enough to do to answer for himself.

You know how it is when you are travelling in a large party; every body wants to help every other body, and yet, as it is, each one has something of his own to carry.

Some time ago I was going down to Mount Desert, in Maine. Among the different parties on the boat, there were seven ladies, old enough to know better, and apparently all of them unmarried, who had one poor young man to take care of them. He bought them their tickets, and checked their trunks, and did every thing for them, and moved, I should say, from eighteen to twenty-five bundles and packages from one end of the boat to the other, according to the view, and the way the sun was shining on those seven upraised parasols. At last, when the boat arrived at Mount Desert, these seven ladies hurried off to the hotel, to secure good rooms, and left this unfortunate young man standing on the wooden pier, with a rampart of bags, shawl-bundles, and satchels around him. He was tall and thin, and his hat-ribbon was waving in the breeze, and at a distance he looked like a flag-staff in the middle of a fortification!

Now I wonder whether St. Paul and St. Luke, and the rest of the apostles, left their baggage for some one else in the party to carry, when they arrived at the wharf at Cæsarea! Did they hurry off to get good rooms in the house of this old disciple of Cyprus, named Mnason, with whom they stopped? And do you suppose when they left his house, they left their bags about for him to gather up and send after them in a wagon? Not a bit of it! St. Paul was too self-reliant a man to do a thing like this. He never wanted other people to carry his bundles. He was a very helpful man. He was always able to take care of himself and then to help others. Besides this, he was a very courteous and polite man. He had been brought up well, and knew what good manners were. He quoted from one of the Grecian poets when he said in his epistle to the Corinthians, "Evil communications corrupt good manners." When he was shipwrecked on the island of Melita he fully appreciated the polite attentions of the chief citizen there, Publius, who, he says, "received us and lodged us three days courteously."

In other words, St. Paul knew how to take the world, and the men and women in the world. He was a great leader of people. And the secret of his great success in life was this, *that he was never above his work.* He says he knew both how to be abased and how to abound; he could go on horseback, or he could go on foot. He could ride in a Roman chariot and talk with Felix and Festus and Agrippa and all the great men, and he could come down to poor Onesimus, the runaway slave, or to the jailer at Philippi, or to those poor women who were always found in the churches which he established.

So, then, we read that the apostles carried their own bundles up to Jerusalem. They had just been on a long missionary journey over the Mediterranean Sea and over Greece and Asia Minor. They were on their way to attend this feast of the old Jewish Church at Jerusalem, and they wanted to go to the city and to their friends there in true missionary style. Like the pilgrim with his staff in his hand and his bag over his shoulder, these brave apostles walked along the highway towards Jerusalem.

I think I can see them now. First, there were the companions whom they met at Cæsarea, the friends of old Mnason from the island of Cyprus. Then, there were those friends of St. Paul whom we like, because we know they were so true to him, but of whom we know so very little: Sopater, a man from Berea, and Gaius, Tychichus, and Aristarchus, and Secundus. Then there were those two young disciples, Timothy and Titus, who were full of their life-work, and were, no doubt, talking of their plans and of the work that was given to them, one at Ephesus and the other in the island of Crete. Then came St. Luke, the beloved physician, and the devoted friend and companion of the apostle Paul; no doubt even then talking with the apostle about what they were to do next. Last of all came the mules and beasts of burden with their drivers, bearing the tents and camp equipage, and all the things they had picked up on their way for the poor Christians at Jerusalem.

I suppose St. Paul's companions who had witnessed some of the stormy events in his life,—when they had been in perils by water and in perils by land, in perils by robbers and in perils by their own countrymen,— couldn't help being anxious about this visit to Jerusalem, especially since the prophet Agabus had told them at Cæsarea, when they landed there, after their voyage, that there was trouble ahead for St. Paul. Perhaps they held back a little; perhaps they walked slowly along the road, and dreaded to turn the corner which showed them in the distance the towers and minarets of Herod's palaces and fortresses; but St. Paul was not afraid. "The will of the Lord be done," was his motto; and I think we can almost feel the military haste and march of this company, in these words by which St. Luke described this event: "And after those days we took up our carriages, and went up to Jerusalem."

So, then, my dear children, don't let any of us be above carrying our own bundles and picking up our own duties. There are some things we can do for others; there are other things which every one must do for himself;—for, after all, every man must bear his own burden.

III.

The third lesson this subject teaches us is this: We must not be afraid of the difficulties in the way.

It is one of the easiest things in the world to discourage people and to get discouraged. If you are going out fishing, and have got every thing ready, and are expecting to have a good time, what a dreadful thing it is to meet some boys on the way back, who laugh and wink at one another, and then tell you they hope you will have lots of bites, and no mosquitoes!

If you are on some mountain climb, and have gone off collecting minerals or specimens of plants, or fern leaves, how discouraging it is to have some one come back just as you are starting out and say, "Don't go; you won't find any thing."

Why, my dear children, the world is full of these discouraging people. They keep saying "*Don't*" all the time. It is don't do this, and don't do that: don't go there, and don't come here: don't try this thing, and don't try that. And it's a hard thing to keep one's will up in the face of all these difficulties and objections. See what St. Paul had to contend with. There were the elders at Miletus who said, "Don't leave us; oh, don't go away from Ephesus"; and there was Agabus at Cæsarea, with the disciples there, who said, "Don't go up to Jerusalem; there will be trouble there if you do. Please don't go." But St. Paul wasn't to be discouraged in this way. He put them all down, and triumphed over them, by his firm and resolute will, when he said: "What mean ye to weep and to break mine heart? for I am ready not to be bound only, but also to die at Jerusalem for the name of the Lord Jesus." That stopped them, and nothing but a firm, resolute will is of any avail in overcoming those who depress and discourage us so.

In "Pilgrim's Progress," Bunyan describes Christian, in one place, as meeting with great difficulties in the way of his taking up his carriages and going on in his path to Jerusalem. Here is the way he describes it; it is the very picture of those who put difficulties in one's path.

"Now when he was got up to the top of the hill, there came two men running amain: the name of the one was Timorous and of the other Mistrust: to whom Christian said, Sirs, what is the matter? You run the wrong way. Timorous answered that they were going to the city of Zion, and had got up that difficult place: but, said he, the farther we go, the more danger we meet with, wherefore we turned, and are going back again.

"Yes, said Mistrust, for just before us lie a couple of lions in the path, whether sleeping or waking we know not: and we could not think if we came within reach, but they would presently pull us in pieces. Then said Christian, you make me afraid; but whither shall I fly to be safe? To go back is nothing but death: to go forward is fear of death and life everlasting beyond it. I will yet go forward! So Mistrust and Timorous ran down the hill and Christian went on his way."

Now, then, my dear children, there are difficulties and trials and duties and burdens in our way all the time. They are like the lions in the path, which frightened back Mistrust and Timorous.

> "There are briers besetting every path,
>   Which call for patient care;
> There is a cross in every lot,
>   And an earnest need for prayer;
> But a lowly heart that leans on thee
>   Is happy anywhere."

Shakespeare, when he is describing Lady Macbeth as striving to arouse her husband's will so that he may murder the old king Duncan, among the other names by which she taunts him, calls him this: "*Infirm of purpose.*" How many of us are infirm of purpose! How many of us turn when we meet with discouragements and discouragers like Mistrust and Timorous! How many of us would have said to Agabus at Cæsarea, "Well, after all, perhaps you are right; it looks so very stormy ahead that we will unpack our trunks and stay here at Cæsarea

Carriages to Jerusalem. 229

awhile. It's so comfortable here. We won't take up our carriages and go up to Jerusalem just at present."

Dear children, don't be *infirm* of purpose when you *know you are right*. Don't be discouraged when you know it is your duty to go on in the way marked out for you. Don't be crowded back from your path of duty, because the discouraging people around you say, "It's no use, don't—don't go on your way to Jerusalem." Rise above it all and say with St. Paul, "What do you mean by all this sort of thing?" and then take up your bundles as he did, and say "Good-by, Cæsarea! good-by, poor old Agabus. You can't frighten me. We're going up to Jerusalem after all."

IV.

The fourth and last lesson this subject teaches us is, that rest comes at the end of the journey.

It wasn't very long before St. Paul was back again at Cæsarea, with a whole troop of Roman soldiers in charge of him. I suppose old Agabus frowned and looked very wise and said, "Just as I expected; just what I told you, Paul!" And it wasn't very long before St. Paul was on his way back to Rome to be tried before the emperor Nero. And the elders at Miletus probably nodded to each other and said, "Just what we said, you know." And then he was set free again, and was back in the old country of Syria once more, before he was taken finally to Rome to be beheaded! His rest was a long way off, but it came at last, when he looked forward with such joy to it, and wrote to his young disciple and companion in travel, Timothy, and said: "I am now ready to be offered, and the time of my departure is at hand." You know that verse of the hymn we sometimes sing:

"Rest comes at length, though life be long and dreary;
 The day must dawn and darksome night be past;
 All journeys end in welcome to the weary,
   And heaven, the heart's true home, will come at last."

What a feeling of rest there is after a long walk, when we have been tramping for miles through the forests and down the mountain-sides, or along the cliffs of the sea-shore, on one of the first cool days of fall. How good it seems to sit before an open fire on the hearth, tired and sleepy, and glowing all over with that feeling of health which comes from the stirred-up blood. We think of the day that is gone, and of all that we have done in it, and then we look forward to the new work of the coming day.

Well, my dear children, I think that is the very picture of the rest of heaven, that rest which remaineth for the people of God. It isn't lazy rest we are to have, but healthful rest; rest that will fit us for the new duties of the other world. It is like the rest and the welcome St. Paul and his companions had when, after carrying their burdens up the high-road to the city's wall, they laid them down at last. For this is the way in which St. Luke describes their arrival: "And when we were come to Jerusalem, the brethren received us gladly."

Sainte-Aldegonde, the great leader of the Netherlanders in their struggle for liberty, the man who carried on the work after William of Orange died, had written upon his shield as his motto, "*Repos Ailleurs*," "Rest elsewhere."

The name of the state of Alabama means, "Here we may rest." When the first settlers in the South drove the Indians into their wildernesses and everglades, one of their chieftains took a party of his tribe miles and miles away from the white men and, driving his tent-pole into the ground, exclaimed, "Alabama," "Here we may rest." But, like a great many other people who drive their stakes firmly down into the soil of this world, he was mistaken.

There is an old legend in church history which says that a Jewish teacher, named Rabbi Judah, and his brethren, the Seven Pillars of Wisdom, sat in the Temple on a feast day, disputing about rest. One said that it was to have attained sufficient wealth, yet without sin; the second, it was fame and praise of all men; the third, it was the possession of power to rule the state; the fourth, that it consisted only in a happy home; the fifth, that it must be in the old age of one who is rich, powerful, famous, surrounded by children's children; the sixth, that all these things were vain unless a man kept all the ritual law of Moses. Then Rabbi Judah said, "Ye have all spoken wisely, but one thing more is necessary; he only can find rest who to all these things addeth this, that he keepeth the traditions of the elders." There sat in the court a fair-haired boy, playing with his lilies in his lap, and hearing the talk, dropped them with astonishment from his hands, looked up and said, "Nay, fathers, he only loveth rest who loves his brother as himself, and God with his whole heart and soul. He is greater than wealth and fame and power, happier than a happy home, happy without it, better than honored age, he is a law to himself and above all tradition." The doctors were astonished. They said, "When Christ cometh shall he tell us greater things?" And yet they did not know that that very child was Christ.

For this doing God's will, after all, is the only true rest which we can have in this world. There is no peace or rest to the wicked; they die with a dread and a terrible fear settling down upon them, as Judas did when he threw down the money and rushed out and hanged himself. They can not have that peace which passeth all understanding; that which the world can not give and can not take away. And it was the knowledge of this rest, and the possession of this peace, which enabled St. Paul to say, "The will of the Lord be done," and then to give the order to his companions for every man to take up his own burden, and not shrink from his duty, and take the "forward-march" step along the highway to Jerusalem.

Remember this text, then, about the carriages to Jerusalem.

Don't forget these lessons: We have all got burdens to carry; every one must carry his own burden; we must not be afraid of the difficulties in the way; and the rest comes at the journey's end.

There is a certain kind of chemical writing which disappears on paper, but which will be brought out when exposed to fire; just so it is with us in learning these lessons in life. I want you to get these truths written in your minds and consciences, and then, by and by, when you get nearer to the fire of life and its reality, the *warm* experiences you may meet there will bring the old writing out.

Pray to Jesus Christ, your Saviour, to make you true, brave boys and girls; ask him to give you strength to do your duty cheerfully in that state of life to which he has been pleased to call you. Don't be afraid of any thing but sin; don't shirk your duties; don't let other people do for you those things you know you ought to do yourself; don't be ashamed or afraid to carry your own burdens; and when you know it is your duty to go right on in the way laid out for you, don't halt on the way, or grumble about the bundles you may have to carry, but say, with the apostles of old, "The will of the Lord be done," and spring to your work.

A little boy was once asked if he wasn't afraid to go through a graveyard at night. He said in reply, "I'm not half as afraid of the dead people as I am of the living, and when I begin to think about it at all, it's a great deal easier and quicker to run *through* the graveyard, than to run *back into* it again."

Be sure you're right, then go ahead; and though others may say I wouldn't, or don't go, or the road's hard, or the sun's hot, rise above them all, as St. Paul did when he bid them all good-by at Cæsarea, and took up his carriages and went up to Jerusalem!

IX.

The Fourfaced Cherubim.
No. 1.—THE FACE OF A LION.

THE FOURFACED CHERUBIM.

I. The Face of a Lion.

"The face of a lion."—Ezekiel i. 10.

THE verse where this text is found is a long and hard one to remember. But I am going to make four sermons out of it, and in this way we will build up its meaning, just as you build up a house out of blocks, with four sides to it.

To-day we are only going to build up one side, and therefore we will only take one fourth part of the whole verse.

We are going, then, to talk about the cherubim, or the strange living creature which the prophet Ezekiel saw in a vision, or dream, when he was a prisoner on the banks of the river Chebar in Chaldea. You know people like to go to shows and museums to see curiosities.

Some time ago Barnum, the great showman, had a woolly horse. Nobody knew where he came from, or any thing about him, but he had wool like a sheep, instead of having short hair like a horse, and ever so many people went to see him. Then he had the Siamese twins, and a woman with a heavy black beard, and giants and dwarfs, and fat boys and thin men, and a happy family of all kinds of animals in a cage together, and a sea-lion, and a whale that was harnessed up to a sort of boat and pulled little Commodore Nutt around in a great tank full of water; and people went to see all these curiosities, just because they were so curious.

Nobody would pay money to see a woolly sheep, or common horses, or cows in a field; or to see a *man* with a beard. We can see these things any day of our lives. But people like to see curious men and women and strange-looking animals, like the hippopotamus, who opens his square jaws at you when the keeper taps him on the mouth with his cane, and then throws his head back and yawns at you out of the water; or the old ourang-outang, or man-monkey, who seems made on purpose to do funny things and make people laugh.

There was a man once, in London, who advertised in the papers, and by handbills on the wall, that he would put himself into a quart bottle. The hall in which he was to perform this wonderful trick was crowded with people many hours before the time of the performance. But of course he could not do it, and when he appeared upon the stage he said that was only his way of bringing crowds of people together to hear a lecture he had.

We all like to hear and see curious men and animals and wonderful things; and now I am going to preach four sermons about this wonderful living creature, with its four faces; this cherubim which the prophet Ezekiel saw.

But here some one may say, "Oh nobody knows what this living creature really was; and how can we find any lesson out of this Bible curiosity?" Now, then, let us see, my dear children, if we can not get four sermons out of this fourfaced cherubim, with plenty of lessons for us all.

Well, then, you know in fairy stories and old legends we continually read about dragons and goblins and great ugly creatures that never existed, and that no one could ever see in the fields or menageries nowadays. In the Apochrypha, or that portion of the Bible between the Old and the New Testament which is not considered the inspired word of God, there is a story about an idol named Bel, and a dragon, which the Babylonians worshipped. This story tells us that Daniel, the same Daniel who was thrown into the den of lions, took pitch and fat and hair, and seethed them together, and made lumps out of them, and put them into the dragon's mouth, so that he burst in two. And yet, even if we don't believe these things we like to read about them. There, for instance, is "Pilgrim's Progress." It is full of stories about giants and monsters and evil spirits; but then we know these things are only

The Fourfaced Cherubim. 243

symbols or images of truth. Then we read in ancient history about the Cyclops, or giant men with one eye in the centre of their foreheads; and about the minotaur, or mammoth bull, in the island of Crete; and about the centaurs, or half men and half horses. But, my dear children, the most wonderful living thing that ever was thought of by any one in fairy story or the old fables, doesn't begin to come near this strange cherubim. Let me tell you about it. Ezekiel, the Jewish prophet, was in captivity in the land of Chaldea, and one day, as he was sitting by the banks of the river Chebar, no doubt thinking about his old home, he had a vision; just as you sometimes fall asleep and have a dream, which seems so real to you that when you awake you can't believe you have only been asleep. Well, Ezekiel had this dream or vision. He saw a whirlwind or cloud of dust come out of the north, and there were dark, heavy clouds and a flame of fire in it. This must have looked like a huge piece of blazing fireworks moving straight across the dark sky. But now listen to the account of this living cherubim in the midst of the flame. I am not going to tell you all that the prophet said about it. That would keep us too long. I shall only tell you a little of what he said. He saw, then, four of these living creatures, and every one had four faces and every one had four wings. The sole of their feet was like the sole of a calf's foot; that is, it was a hoof. They had the hands of a man under their wings on their four sides. Two wings were joined together and two wings covered their bodies. Then there were wheels and rings and burning brass and coals of fire and smoke. They went like a flash of lightning across the heavens. Moreover, they had four faces, the face of a lion, the face of an ox, the face of an eagle, and the face of a man.

Now there are two other places in the Bible where we read about this cherubim. One is in the book of Exodus, where Moses tells us how Bezaleel, the man who made the ark, or chest, of the covenant, carved out two cherubim, with wings touching each other, over the Holy Place. The other is in the book of the Revelation of St. John (some people call it "Revelations," but that is wrong), where we read about four living creatures who were before the throne of God. There we read that the first beast, or living creature, was like a lion, the second was like a calf, the third had the face of a man, and the fourth was like a flying eagle. This is all that the Bible tells us about the cherubim. It must have been a very curious and mysterious being. We can not imagine how it looked, or know all that it was meant to teach the prophet Ezekiel. But it teaches us all one great lesson. It is this. God wants his children to be full of life and activity for him. He does not want any laziness, either here on earth or among his angels in heaven. He does not want the living beings who are to be around his throne, and are to do his will, to be sleepy, onesided creatures. He wants them to be full of life and activity: as full of it as children are when they are let out of school at recess-time; as full as a Leyden jar is, when it is charged and filled with electricity. The cherubim, as it went flashing through the heavens, had four kinds of life in it: the life the lion leads; the life the ox leads; the life the eagle leads, and the life of man.

And in this same way God wants us to have in our characters and lives the face, or the character, of the lion; the face, or likeness, of the ox; the face of the eagle, as well as the character of man. This, then, is the lesson which the prophet's vision of the wonderful cherubim teaches us.

Now we come to-day, in this first sermon about the fourfaced cherubim, to the first of these faces—the face of the lion. And this face of the lion teaches us two lessons.

First. It teaches us a lesson of *activity.*
Some animals are quiet and do not move about much. Look at the cattle in a field. They move about slowly; they always walk just as if they were to live forever. They do

not run about a field as horses do. There is an animal in South America called the sloth, simply because he is so lazy. He curls himself up in a tree, and never moves except when he can not help moving. In the Zoölogical garden out at Fairmount Park, in Philadelphia, there is a large bird-house filled with all sorts of birds. There are eagles and hawks and great vultures, who fly about all over the place; and up in the trees you will see a whole family of owls, who appear never to move off their perches, but sit all day and do nothing but blink their eyes.

Animals have character in their faces just as truly as men and women have. The bear tells you by his look that he is sullen; the fox tells you that he is sly; the mule says by his looks, "I am obstinate," just as truly as if this was labelled on him, like the labels of an apothecary; the ox tells you he is patient and quiet, and the lion, as he moves through the desert, or paces up and down his cage, has the look of a creature that is active and brave. The lion knows perfectly well all the ground about his den. He goes over it in the night-time. Sometimes he goes for many miles, in order to know every tree and swamp and hollow place, just as a gardener knows all about his garden. He sleeps in the day-time, and roars and travels about at night, in order to hunt his food. And he goes his rounds as regularly as the hands of a clock go round its face; just as carefully as a watchman, or a policeman, goes on his beat at night.

Goats and sheep and rabbits are active, but this is only when they feel like it; they have no such regularity about their lives as the lion has in his business-like activity. Some time ago I went down into the vaults of one of our great safe-deposit buildings. You know people buy and hire boxes or drawers in these vaults, where they keep their valuables. Sometimes it is jewelry they have; sometimes it is papers and precious documents, which they put in these drawers for safekeeping. The president of the institution went along and showed me

The Fourfaced Cherubim. 249

the place where the watchman walked every night. At the end of every hour he has to be at a certain place where there is a watch to be wound up, and if he is not in that part of the building to wind it up at the proper time, it will be a tell-tale to him in the morning, and will let the superintendent know that he has not done his duty. It will not do for him merely to walk up and down one side of the place, he must walk all the way round. He mustn't frisk about only when he feels like going, as the goats do when they are active; he must be regular in his activity, as the lion is.

And, my dear children, we should try to be like the lion in this respect. How many people there are in the world who don't know what to do with themselves. They are not very much in earnest about things of this world; they are not in earnest about the world to come. They live, like butterflies, or foolish grasshoppers, who have a good time to-day, but take no thought of the morrow. They call having a good time "killing time," as if time was an enemy; forgetting that hymn so dear to the Christian heart, which says,

> " And fast as my minutes roll on
> They bring me but nearer to thee."

These kind of people are active enough, but what do they have to show at the end of the year? The year is burned out just as a candle burns,—sputters, flickers, and goes out. People in the world are active, but how few there are who have the lion's resolute, systematic, determined activity. He is a great, noble, kingly beast. David says in one of the psalms, "The lions roaring after their prey do seek their meat from God." There is nothing trifling or small about the lion. He sets us a great example in his activity. It is his business to support himself and his family on the lower animals, just as we pay our butchers to kill sheep and oxen and poultry for us. He does not delight in playing with his victims, as the tiger and the cat do. He is thoroughly in earnest in his business of killing. He kills his enemies like a kingly warrior, in an open and fair way. In Africa the Hottentots try all kinds of ways to catch him, by laying snares for him. But he does not seem to surprise them by lying in wait for them. If they come in his way, he will fight, but he won't go out of his way for them. They know his habits and they watch for him. They know he will not stay in his den doing nothing, or crawling about like a sneak-thief. They know he is a regular watchman, treading his rounds at regular times, and so they watch for him and kill him. And the "face of the lion" in this wonderful cherubim, as it went flying across the sky, means this same prompt and regular activity. God wants all his children to be thoroughly alive for him. The angels crowd around God's throne and fly to do his will. They love to do it; they are in a *hurry to do it*. Just think of that, now! How many of you hurry, not to your kite, marbles, or base-ball grounds, but how many of you hurry to run errands for your parents? Well, the angels are God's messengers; they go on his holy errands; they never say, "I am going, presently"; they are gone before they know it. Why, look at the archangel Gabriel. God told him to take a message to the prophet Daniel in Babylon, and he went, oh, how quickly! There was the face of the lion about him when he went flying through space, just as the cherubim went. He passed by other worlds and suns and systems, he flew through all the stars of the milky way, and came at last within sight of the planet Earth. It must have seemed just like a speck to him at the first. Then it grew larger and larger, until the shadow of the light made it appear darker and darker; and at last, as Daniel himself says, about the time of the evening oblation, or prayer-time, the man Gabriel whom he had seen before, in a vision, touched him on the shoulder, and told him that he had come with a message from God in answer to his prayer. Think how swiftly Gabriel must have flown to do God's will, and carry the

The Fourfaced Cherubim. 253

message to his servant, all the way from Heaven to Babylon.

This, then, is the first lesson which the face of the lion teaches us. God wants us to be active for him. He gives us eyes to see with, ears to hear with, hands to handle with, feet to walk with, and he wants all these to be used for him. You know if we don't use a thing it will spoil. If you buy a wooden bucket which is made on purpose to hold water, and then put it in the sun without any water in it, it will come to pieces. If you keep only a very little water in a large tin which is meant to hold a great deal of water, it will rust the tin. If you build a locomotive, or a steamboat, and then let them stand in the sun and the rain without ever using the machinery, it will rust to pieces. And, just in the same way, there are many people who tie up all their good traits of character, as old Egyptian mummies are strapped and bandaged together. Their souls go to rust, they wither away and shrivel up, because they are not active for God, and have not any thing to do for him.

Remember, then, that activity is the first thing which the face of the lion teaches us.

The second lesson which the face of the lion teaches us is—*Courage.*

We all like to read about brave, strong men. Look at King Richard the First. They called him Cœur de Leon, or "Him of the Lion Heart." He swung a tremendous battle-axe, and was a terrible fellow, as he came tearing down among the Mohammedans with their thin linen turbans. But then this is not the greatest kind of strength. They used to think so in olden times. The man who could shake the heaviest lance or spear, or throw the largest stone, or wear the heaviest armor, was considered the greatest man. And when two armies met, they fought just like wild beasts. One army would stand up and cut the other army into pieces, just as a butcher cuts up chops upon a meat-block.

But as the world has become more and more Christianized, men have found out that there is something better than mere animal strength. The world has found out that there is some better way of settling disputes than by merely fighting over the question. The pen is mightier than the sword, and moral courage, or the strength to do right, is a great deal better than merely animal courage.

There are plenty of men who would stand up on a battle-field where the shots are whizzing and the great cannon-balls are flying, who would be afraid to stand up for the right, if it was an unpopular thing to do; or to be owned as a disciple of the Lord Jesus, if their friends and comrades laughed at them.

Some years ago, in Kentucky, there was a brave, rough old revival preacher, named Peter Cartwright. He used to preach just what he believed, and was never afraid of speaking out his mind. One day General Jackson, who was then a candidate for the presidency, went to church to hear him preach. Just as the old minister was about to announce his text, one of the elders of the church walked up into the pulpit, and whispered in his ear that since they had so great a man present as General Jackson, he had better not preach as plainly as usual. Old Peter Cartwright heard the elder through, and then answered back in a loud tone, so that every one in the church could hear, "What do I care for General Jackson. He will be lost just like any other sinner if he don't repent and love Jesus Christ."

In the days of Louis XI., of France, there was a brave old monk, named Millard, who used to rebuke the king in public for his vices. One day while he was preaching to a crowd of people in Paris, a messenger from the king with half a dozen of the royal guard appeared on the scene to stop him. The messenger told him that the king said if he didn't change his tone he would have him thrown into the river Seine. "Tell him," replied the old monk, "that I will get to heaven sooner by water than he with all his post-horses." And the crowd would not let the soldiers hurt the preacher.

Here is one story more. In the days of the Roman republic there was a celebrated king and warrior named Pyrrhus. He was king of a little country called Epirus, which was a part of Greece. He was very anxious to get the Romans over to his side in a war which he was then waging. The Romans sent out an ambassador to him named Fabricius. The Roman people at that time were very plain and simple in their way of living, for Rome was a republic something like the United States, only they had two presidents at a time, whom they called consuls. Pyrrhus thought he would do all in his power to make a great effect upon the ambassador's mind and gain him over to his side. So the first day he spent in the camp of Pyrrhus, a grand entertainment was given in his honor. The plain Roman had never before seen so much grandeur and such style of living. There were so many things to eat and drink, and such splendid cups and vessels of silver and gold, that he could hardly eat any thing. At last when it was all over, some Ethiopian slaves appeared, bringing the ambassador quantities of presents of gold and silver plate and vessels. But Fabricius declined them all, saying he was not allowed by his government to receive any presents. The next day Pyrrhus thought to himself, "Now I'll frighten him into my terms." The Grecians used to fight in those days with elephants, and it appeared that Fabricius had never seen an elephant. So while they were dining together on the second day, all of a sudden a dreadful noise was heard; the screens which were around the table disappeared, and three large elephants, with torches in their trunks, marched up to the table, and flamed their lights about. It had been arranged by Pyrrhus that when the elephants should appear, he and his guests should run, as if in terror. But Fabricius sat at his place, with the elephants marching around the pavilion, and only remarked to

Pyrrhus when he returned, "You no more frighten me with your beasts to-day, than you moved me with your bribes yesterday."

My dear children, we may not have great strength of body, as the lion has, but we can have, in our way, something of his splendid courage. We can stand up against sin and temptation, and have moral courage not to be afraid to do right, as the lion has courage not to yield, but to die fighting. When Louis XVI., king of France, was taken prisoner in the beautiful palace of the Tuilleries by the infuriated mob who put him to death on the guillotine, he had a body-guard of soldiers, known as the Swiss Guard, who stood to the very last defending the palace, and died, fighting till there wasn't one left.

And the great sculptor Thorwalsden, cut out of a rock at Lucerne in Switzerland in memory of these brave men, a mammoth lion, pierced with an arrow and dying, and yet with his noble great paw holding on to the French shield, and trying to cling to it to the very last.

Think how the martyrs went joyfully to death for the love they bore to their Lord. They didn't think about their tortures or the pain of dying. In the eleventh chapter of the epistle to the Hebrews there is a long account of the faith and courage of God's servants. There we read, "They were stoned, they were sawn asunder, were tempted, were slain with the sword: they wandered about in sheepskins and goatskins; being destitute, afflicted, tormented." But they knew God would take their souls from their burning bodies; they knew they would look down on their poor bodies tied to the hot stake, just as Elijah looked down from his chariot of fire, taking him straight to God, upon poor Elisha, who was left behind. If we are only Christians, we ought not to be afraid of any thing but sin. We oughtn't to fear death. Jesus said, "Fear not him who killeth the body, and after that hath no more power to hurt. But I will forewarn you whom ye shall fear. Fear him who after he has killed you, hath power to cast both body and soul in hell. Yea, I say unto you, fear him." That is, we must be afraid of Satan's power and our own sinful, evil wills.

And now let me close this sermon with one story more, a story I heard once when I was a little boy, and which I have never forgotten, and which I do not want you to forget.

There was some time ago in England, a dear old clergyman, who had a beautiful rural church, very old and overgrown with ivy. His daughter used to teach a class of boys in church, long before there was any thing like our present Sunday-schools. Every one loved the dear old minister, he was so good and kind. Sometimes he used to come into church before service time, and tell the different classes stories. The children would watch to see the old man coming, and then some of them would run along the shaded path that led to the church porch to meet him and take his hand, and beg him to come and tell *their* class a story. And the old man would pat them on the head, and kiss the little ones, and say, "Well, well! Let me see, whose turn is it now?"

One Sunday afternoon it came round to his daughter's turn to have a story, and when the boys were all around him, he leaned his chin on his cane and told them this story:

"One very warm afternoon, as I was sitting in my study window, I heard you children coming along to church, and I fell asleep with your voices ringing in my ear. I dreamed that I was in a boat all alone; the water was very rough and boisterous, and the sky was angry and stormy, and I was afraid I would go down. Suddenly, it seemed as if some angel took hold of my little boat, for in a few minutes I found myself in perfectly still water. I was in a coral grove; the water was calm and blue, and I could look far down into the depths below, and see the pearl shells down there on the reef. I saw children playing upon the shore; they were dressed in white, and each one had a red sash around his waist and a silver cross around his neck. I heard a bell ringing in the distance, and saw the children going into church. 'What place is this?' I asked, as the children came flocking around my boat on the sand. 'This is the Island Home of the Good Shepherd,' said a tall boy named Angelo. 'We are all under the care of a dear teacher named Pastor. Once we belonged to a wicked master, but our Good Shepherd died to save us from his power, and Pastor teaches us all about heaven and sin and the life everlasting. We wear this blood-red sash, because the Good Shepherd shed his blood for us. We wear this cross around our necks, because it is the sign that we are his faithful soldiers and servants. But here come Pastor and Guido and Stephen, our three teachers.' And I was welcomed by them all, and went with them into church. Then after service, they showed me the school-room, and the garden where the children worked, and I stayed with them, as it seemed to me, many days.

"But I saw they were not all obedient to Pastor, though Angelo, the oldest boy, tried hard to set them a good example. I saw three boys named Wayward and Slothful and Timid, who pouted about the work they had to do, and spoke cross words to Angelo when he reproved them.

"'We don't want to work: we want to have a good time; what's the use in minding such hard rules? Why can't we do as we want?'

"'That's so,' said a voice from a boat near by, for they were standing by a curve in the shore. 'That's so, get in my boat and we will go a-fishing; I am a fisherman.'

"'No,' said a little girl named Bella, 'you haven't any sash, and you haven't any cross, and Pastor told us never to listen to any one who tempted us to go away.'

"'Who cares for such things,' said the fisherman. 'Jump in! Jump in!'

"'Let us go,' replied Wayward, and he and Slothful put Timid and little Bella in the boat, and they pushed off.

"There was a fine, large, noble-looking boy standing near them, named Courage. When he saw what was done, he ran to the boathouse, where there was a large bell, and rang it violently, with all his might. This soon brought all the boys together.

"'Boys,' cried Courage, 'who'll go with me after that villain of a fisherman? He is a servant of our old master the evil one; see he is frightening the children now. And as he said this, they heard the black fisherman laughing and shouting, 'Now I have caught you! Now I have caught you!' Then he rocked the boat so wildly that they almost fell in the water! After this, he took off their silver crosses and their red sashes, and put them in his pocket.

"But none of the older boys were near enough to go with Courage. Angelo and Stephen were in the garden, and the little boys were afraid to go. So Courage, very quickly, pushed out a boat for himself, and rowed as fast as he could. In the meantime the little boys went on ringing the bell, and Pastor and the teachers came running down to the point. There they saw Courage, all alone, chasing the fisherman. But he rowed so hard that he did not see that the fisherman changed the direction of his boat, and was rowing right into the side of his boat, to swamp him. Suddenly, there was a crash! Courage was thrown backwards; the boat filled with water and sank, and Courage was struggling alone in the water. The fisherman rowed forward laughing at Courage, and calling out to him to catch him. Wayward and Timid and Slothful were tied in the bottom of the boat, and though they screamed for help, it was all in vain.

"'Take me, Courage! Dear Courage, take me!' cried little Bella, and she jumped into the water.

"Courage swam up to her, and told her to put her arms around his neck and hold on to him. Then he began to swim back. In the mean time, Stephen and Guido and Angelo and the boatmen pulled out in the other boats, and rowed hard and fast to reach Courage. But it was too late! He was too much exhausted. He gave out.

He went under twice, and poor little Bella fell off, but was caught by the nearest boatman, while Courage sank for the third time in the water, and was drowned.

"They found his body and brought it ashore, and when they were weeping loudest, and the boat-house bell was tolling, I sighed a long sigh, and—found it was only a dream.

"I heard the church bell ring, and had just time to hurry into service. But I couldn't forget about the Island Home all that day, and I kept thinking about dear, brave Courage all through my sermon.

"And now, boys," said the old minister, "your teacher will explain this story to you."

Well, it isn't hard to do this.

The Christian Church where we are taught the truth about our Saviour is our Island Home; and if we are trying to be Christians, then we are like these children who had the silver cross around their necks.

Remember that Satan is near you, to tempt you into sin, as the fisherman tempted Wayward. Remember he finds mischief still for idle hands to do.

Therefore, be lion-like: be active; be courageous; be strong in doing good; be strong in resisting temptation. Remember that "the wicked flee when no man pursueth, but the righteous are bold as the lion."

This fourfaced cherubim, then, teaches us that God wants his children to be full of life for him. He doesn't want us to be onesided merely. And the face of the lion means that we should be like the lion, in being active and in being brave.

We can all be very courageous for Jesus, and for the right, if we pray to God to help us.

Pray, then, dear children, that God may give you the face of the lion in your character; that you may have the lion's *activity*, and the lion's *courage!*

X.
The Fourfaced Cherubim.
No. 2.—THE FACE OF AN OX.

THE FOURFACED CHERUBIM.

II. The Face of an Ox.

"The face of an ox."—Ezekiel i. 10.

THIS face of the ox was on the left side of the cherubim. The face of the man and the face of the lion were on the right-hand side. We don't know just where the face of the eagle was placed. It must have been a very wonderful living creature, as the prophet Ezekiel saw it flying over the plains. As we have seen before, these same four faces appear in St. John's vision of heaven. Before the throne of God, there were four living creatures, and the first was like a lion, and the second was like a calf, and the third beast had a face as a man, and the fourth beast was like a flying eagle.

All forms of life were represented in heaven

by these four appearances, of the lion, the ox, the eagle, and the man, and it was all these different kinds of life in one living creature which the Jewish prophet saw, when he beheld in his vision this strange and mysterious cherubim.

We learn from this second face in the cherubim to have the power or the endurance of the ox. And the ox represents two kinds of power: *power to do*, and *power to suffer*.

I.

First, then:

Power to do, or strength to work. This is the first thing the face, or the character, of the ox means. The ox is trained to do his work; he does not come to it naturally. Calves and colts are led by ropes and halters before they are put into shafts. They have strength when they are young; but it does not amount to any thing, because it is untrained strength. They play in the fields, while the patient oxen are pulling under the heavy yoke, which seems so hard and uncomfortable, and the steady old plough-horses are dragging the heavy traces of the plough, or working along in the big, thick shafts of the rough old cart. And the oxen turn their big bull necks and suffering looking eyes at them, and the old horses turn their heads, and look out from their hard leathern blinders at them, capering about in the pasture, as much as to say, "Never mind, you gay little chaps, your time for working will come by and by!"

This strength which the ox and the horse have is *trained* strength. See how long it takes to break them in. An ox will try for a month to wriggle his head out of a yoke, and a colt will chew on his bit for weeks, before he learns to give up and submit to his fate.

Why, to hear a man drive oxen and talk to them, one would think that it required a very long time to break them in, and get them accustomed to the language. The drivers of ox-carts have long poles, and they keep touching the oxen on the heads all the time, and calling out, "Haw, buck, gee! Oh, haw! Whoa, buck!" etc. It sounds just like reading Hebrew out aloud! But the oxen become accustomed to it in some way, and will not pull well unless they are talked to; though I should think it would make them mad to be talked to so incessantly.

And you and I, my dear children, have our training-days, just as the young oxen have theirs. We have got to put some yoke on one of these days; we have got to pull in some kind of shafts. I know how boys feel about going to school. They think — "Oh, dear me! I wish I didn't have to work so hard, and go to school every morning, year in and year out. I wish I could be free, like my father." But, my dear children, work is the law of this world. Even Jesus, when he was on earth, said, "My Father worketh hitherto, and I work." None of us can do just as we want to do all the time; and it wouldn't be well for us if we could. "No man liveth unto himself." *We have got to put on the yoke some time.*

We may fuss and fume about it, as the colts do; or we may try to wriggle out of it, as the young oxen do; but one of these days we'll give up trying to get out of it, and then we will be trained.

Now this may look hard, but in reality it isn't hard. We were made to work: the face of the ox means power to work, or strength to act, and we ought to have this power of doing something, or of working, in our lives. You and I were made to work, just as the ox was made for the yoke, and the yoke was made for the ox.

Some boys go into stores, and enter upon business; some study in lawyers' offices, and become lawyers themselves; some go into the army, some into the navy, some study medicine, and a very few become ministers.

And if all these boys want to succeed in life, in their different callings, they must see to it that they are thoroughly broken in, and are carefully trained for the work before them. They must be willing to wear the yoke of patient service if they want to succeed. They mustn't be afraid of the yoke and the yoke-pins; they must have the face of the ox; they must have strength to labor, ability to do a good day's work.

In some of our geography books there are pictures at the head of the lessons, representing the progress of our country in civilization. Indians on their little ponies, and great, shaggy, plunging buffaloes, are running away further west before railroad cars and steamboats, and farmers who are cutting down trees and ploughing the ground with a lot of oxen. Now what is the difference between the Indian and the white man? What is the difference between the buffaloes and the oxen? Simply the *difference of the yoke*. The white men and the oxen are trained, they are civilized; the Red men and the buffaloes are uncivilized. They have never been trained. They haven't got the face of the ox in their lives. This is very wonderful; but it is the strength which has come out of discipline, and out of training, which has given this great continent of

North America to the white men, or the Anglo-Saxon race, as we are called in the books.

And then, too, when we come to the thought of being strong Christians, and serving God, we find that there are just the same two classes of people: the trained and the untrained; or those who have strength to do something for him, and those who have no willingness or power to work for him.

After all that we may say about it, there are only two great masters in the world: these are Jesus Christ and Satan. The two ways of being trained are by doing the will of our Father in heaven, and by doing our own will; and the two yokes are the yoke of duty and the yoke of pleasure. Our Saviour once said to the people that were about him, "Come unto me, all ye that labor and are heavy laden, and I will give you rest. Take my yoke upon you, and learn of me; for I am meek and lowly in heart: and ye shall find rest unto your souls. For my yoke is easy, and my burden is light."

In the year 273 there was a famous emperor of Rome named Aurelian. In the midst of his wars and conquests he overthrew a celebrated queen named Zenobia. Her husband's name was Odenatus. He built up a kingdom over in Syria, and founded a city called Palmyra. When Odenatus died, Zenobia, his wife, ruled, and called herself Queen of the East. You can read all about her wonderful kingdom, one of these days, in Gibbon's "History of the Decline and Fall of the Roman Empire."

Well, the great emperor Aurelian stormed the city and destroyed the temples and made Zenobia his captive. She was a very proud and haughty woman, and she tried very hard to kill herself rather than be compelled to walk after Aurelian's chariot when he had his final triumph in the streets of Rome. The captives used to have to walk, with chains on them, after their conqueror's chariots. When Aurelian saw how proud she was, and how she took on about following after his chariot as a captive, he ordered her

The Fourfaced Cherubim. 279

chains to be made of gold; and so this queenly woman, with her crown on her head and with gold chains about her body, followed her great conqueror.

Children, were those chains any less chains, —any the less strong fetters,—binding that captive woman to the triumphal chariot of Aurelian, because they were of gold? Of course not. They were chains, even if they were made of gold.

Well, just in this same way, Satan's chains are made; his yoke doesn't look like a hard yoke, but it is hard, after all, even though it is stuffed and padded with this world's soft things. His chains don't look like chains, because they are bright and shiny; but the gilt will wear off some day, and the soft paddings in his yoke will all disappear, and then we will be as much his captives, after all, as Zenobia, the Queen of the East, was the captive of the emperor Aurelian.

And you and I, my dear children, are training now to serve one of these two masters.

In fact we are already serving Satan, if

we are not now serving Christ. Jesus said, "He that is not with me is against me, and he that gathereth not with me scattereth abroad." He wants us all to do our heavenly Father's will: not to be wild and sinful and untrained, doing only our own will, just what we happen at the moment to want to do. He wants us to put on the yoke of service for God, just as he himself came down from heaven not to do his own will, but the will of him that sent him; just as he came not to be ministered unto, but to minister and to give his life a ransom for many. He wants us to be trained for his service, because it is our duty to do it, and because we will be the happier for it.

We ought to have, then, the face, or the likeness, of the ox in our characters; we ought to have his trained power to work, and to pull on the side of Jesus in this busy, struggling, wicked world.

We must not think, then, that we have nothing to do for him, because he has done every thing for us; that we can have any

ROMAN GLADIATORS SALUTING THE EMPEROR.
W. Gate.

"reserved seats" in his service, and look on at others doing all the work.

In the old Roman amphitheatre, in the days when they used to have those terribly cruel sports known as gladiatorial shows, the poor gladiators, with their shields and helmets on, would march up in a sad sort of funeral procession to the throne of the emperor, knowing that some of them would never come out of that same ring alive, and would brandish their swords before him, saying, "*Ave Cæsarem: morituri te salutant.*" And then, while the emperor and the coliseum packed with thousands of people would look on at the combat, these men would fight for their lives, until one or the other side were all killed.

Now suppose you and I had to fight in this way for our own salvation, suppose we could not be saved unless we fought in the ring with some combatants there, how much harder it would be for us to be saved!

But suppose, now, that while these gladiators were getting ready for their contest in the ring, the great emperor himself should come down from his throne and say, "I will take these men's places; I will fight for them, and they shall go free." Oh, what a shout of praise and gratitude those poor doomed men would raise!

And yet this is just what God has done for us. Here is what the prophet, speaking by the inspiration of the Holy Spirit, says, as if it were God himself who was speaking: "I have trodden the winepress alone, and of the people there was none with me; and I looked and there was none to help; and wondered that there was none to uphold: therefore mine own arm brought salvation unto me, and my fury it upheld me. For he said, Surely they are my people, children that will not lie, so he was their Saviour. In all their affliction he was afflicted, and the Angel of his presence saved them; in his love and in his pity he redeemed them; and he bare them, and carried them all the days of old."

Once the great Dr. Livingstone, the missionary and explorer of Africa, was writing home from one of his encampments about some of the trials and privations he met with in his journeyings, and then ended his letter with these words: "But these privations are not mentioned as if I considered them in the light of sacrifice. I think that word 'sacrifice' ought never to be used with reference to any thing we can do for him who though he was rich, yet for our sakes became poor."

What we want, then, is trained strength for Christ's service; not in order to save ourselves, but to show our thankfulness to our Saviour for all that he has done for us. We want to be trained for our Lord's yoke, that we may do something for him; we want to have the first thing the face of the ox tells us we ought to have—*Power to work.*

II.

Power to suffer is the other kind of power the face of the ox teaches us.

The ox not only labors in the field in the plough; he yields up his life upon the altar.

In the old Jewish worship oxen were sacrificed continually upon the brazen altar; and to-day there are no animals which are killed so frequently for man's food as oxen. Thus they stand as a type, or picture, of sacrifice and submission. And we must learn to submit, and to give up our own wills, and be patient.

When John Milton, the great English poet, became blind, he wrote a poem about the darkness and loneliness he was in through this great affliction, and it ended with these words, speaking of God's manifold kingdom:

> "———his state
> Is kingly: thousands at his bidding speed
> And post o'er land and ocean without rest.
> They also serve who only stand and wait."

It is a great deal harder for soldiers to stand idly by upon a battle-field, not fighting, but only waiting for their time to come. At the battle of Waterloo, Napoleon's Old Guard could not stand it, and they cried out—"Let us go! Let us go! Don't keep us waiting."

And King Solomon says in the book of Proverbs, "He that ruleth his temper is better than he that taketh a city." That is, it is better to stand by, and hold and curb one's self, and stand being stormed, than it is to storm at another man.

Sir Walter Raleigh was once challenged by a hot-headed young man to fight, and because he refused, the young man spit in his face, as the Jews did to Jesus. Now Sir Walter Raleigh was a great discoverer; he had been over the waters to America and the East Indies, and had served in the army, and wasn't afraid of any thing or any body. But he tried hard to be a true Christian, and on this occasion, showing this power which the ox has,—power to suffer,—he simply took out his handkerchief, and calmly wiping off his face, made this reply: "Young man, if I could as easily wipe your blood from my conscience as I can this injury from my face, I would shoot this very minute, here on this spot."

And this strength to submit, this power

which will enable us to suffer for a cause when we can not do any thing else for it, is a very hard thing to get. This is what St. Peter has in mind, when he says, "This is thankworthy, if a man for conscience toward God endure grief, suffering wrongfully. For what glory is it, if, when ye be buffeted for your faults, ye shall take it patiently? but if, when ye do well, and suffer for it, ye take it patiently, this is acceptable with God. For even hereunto were ye called: because Christ also suffered for us, leaving us an example, that ye should follow his steps: who did no sin, neither was guile found in his mouth." But here some one may say,—"Oh, this is a very hard thing to do, and only saints and martyrs can do it; and, after all, God gives his great big saints strength enough for their sufferings, but he can't expect much of us children, in these days."

But, my dear children, God is not a hard master, and he don't want us to do impossible things! But he does want us to try to do something, or to suffer something, for him. Look at the disciples. Once when Jesus was with them, there was a great multitude of people listening to him in a desert place, and they had nothing to eat, and many of them came a great distance. Then Jesus said to Philip, "Whence shall we buy bread that these may eat?" Philip thought that if they had two hundred penny-worth of bread it would not be enough. Then Andrew, Simon Peter's brother, said there was a boy in the company who had five barley loaves and two fishes. Jesus said that would do. I wonder whether they bought it of him, or whether he gave it. I always thought this boy gave it; that when he saw they hadn't any thing to eat he ran up to Jesus, saying, "Here's some bread, and here are some fishes; take them, if they are of any use." That boy went without his bread, and the fishes he had just caught; he gave them to Jesus, and Jesus blessed them, and blessed the boy, and made his gift the means of doing a wonderful work in feeding the five thousand people. Jesus didn't ask that boy to give him five thousand loaves, he only asked him for five; that was enough for him, that was enough to work the miracle with. And he don't want you, my dear children, to do impossible things: to jump into the fire, or into the water for his sake. He only wants you boys and girls, who are trying to be his children, to be willing to submit now and then for his sake: not to do always just what you want to do, but to have this kind of power the ox has—power to bear, power to submit.

In school, in your plays, at home, when things don't go just as you want, then try to remember how your Saviour "when he was reviled, reviled not again; when he suffered he threatened not, but committed himself to him that judgeth righteously:" that is, to God his Father, who knew every thing about his whole life. And that is what I mean by our having this second kind of strength: strength to suffer, to submit patiently, as the face of the ox tells us he submits.

There was in a Sunday-school in Manchester, England, a poor little girl named Polly. She had a hard, careless mother who made no account of religion, and was sometimes very rough and cruel to her child. One Sunday morning, at breakfast time, her mother said to her,

"Heighho, Polly, run to the shop and get us a loaf for breakfast and a jug of beer.

"Why, mother," said the girl, "it's Sunday!"

"And what if it is," replied her mother. "Dost think we mun have no breakfast because it's a Sunday?"

Poor little Polly was about to say that the loaf might have been got on Saturday, when her mother, who perceived she was going to "praich a sarmunt," stopped all further inquiries on the subject by hitting the girl some heavy blows on the back, and then going to fetch the loaf herself. Polly cried, not so much about the blows as to see her mother behave so, and her grief was by no means diminished when her mother returned and said she could have no breakfast, because she would not get the loaf. Polly said nothing, but quietly went off to school. This was only the beginning of Polly's troubles, for on her return home to dinner she had hardly entered the house, when her mother declared she was a little canting Methodist and should have no dinner, for not bringing the loaf in the morning. Poor girl, what was she to do! First she thought she would run away to her grandmother's, and never go home again; then she thought she would go right off and tell her Sunday-school teacher all about it. But she did not do either of these. She went right up in her own little room, up the dark rickety stairs, in the attic. She untied her bonnet, and took off her shawl, and dropped on her knees by the bedside. "Oh, God!" she said, "help a poor, feeble, little girl to bear up under all this! I'm hungry, and I'm weak, and I'm almost broken-hearted. Help me. Thou hast meat that my mother knows not of. Give me some." And then she prayed for her mother, that God would touch her heart. And when she got up from her knees, though she was so faint that she could hardly hold up her head, she put on her things again and crept quietly down-stairs and off to school. Her mother eyed her as she passed, and she saw a calmness in her white face, and a resignation in her eyes, red with weeping, that went to her very soul. Her teacher at the Sunday-school saw that there was something the matter with Polly, but she could not get out of her what it was. She sat in her class, and looked at her teacher with her pale face, and listened to all that she said. Polly was as ready as any to answer questions, and she almost forgot her mother's treatment of her and her own hunger. But as she was walking home she was almost ready to stop with feebleness, and when she entered the doorway and her mother saw her, the true motherly feelings prevailed; she was subdued by her poor child's quiet, patient suffering.

"Oh, Polly!" she said, "how sorry I am that I've kept thee starving all day. Polly, dear, you will forgive me. Won't you Polly?" And then she asked if she had had any thing to eat and whether she had told any one about it.

Thus little Polly, the poor, weak child, got the victory; not by resistance, but by submission; not by the power of doing, but by the power of bearing; and she was never treated unkindly by any one at home again.

Many years ago there was a missionary society among the Moravians. These Moravians sent out a great many missionaries into this country. A certain nobleman, named Count Zinzendorf, was at the head of this society. And the seal of this society, the stamp that was made upon all their documents and papers, was a picture of an ox standing between an altar and a plough, with this motto underneath:

"Ready for Either."

The plough means labor, or power to work; and the altar means sacrifice, or power to submit; and the face of the ox standing between the plough and the altar means the two kinds of power, of which we have been speaking in this sermon:

Power to do.

Power to suffer.

This is just the place where every true Christian ought to stand: willing to work, or willing to suffer, as God sees fit.

Bear in mind, then, the two kinds of power the face of the ox teaches us, and let us try always to be—

"*Ready for either.*"

XI.
The Fourfaced Cherubim.
No. 3.—THE FACE OF AN EAGLE.

THE FOURFACED CHERUBIM.

III. THE FACE OF AN EAGLE.

"The face of an eagle."—EZEKIEL i. 10.

WE come now to the third face in this wonderful cherubim, "the face of an eagle."

Just as the lion seems to be the king among the beasts of the field, so the eagle seems to be the king of all the birds. You know we Americans are very proud of the eagle. It is stamped upon our gold and silver coins, and helps to form our national coat of arms. You have all seen this splendid American eagle in these pictures, defending the stars and stripes, and looking very fierce with his stretched-out neck and sharp beak and the sharp arrows in his claws, or talons. Then, in ancient history, we know the Roman soldiers used to have golden eagles put upon rods, in the place of flags and banners, and they used to fight in battle to defend these eagles, just as soldiers nowadays fight over their flags, and die rather than give up their colors. In the pictures of Roman battles and triumphal marches you will see these rods with eagles at the top of them, while underneath the eagles you will see a square sort of bar (something like this) with these letters on it,

These letters are for the following Latin words— "*Senatus Populus que Romanus,*" and mean, "The Senate and People of Rome." Then, too, the French soldiers since the time of Napoleon have had golden eagles along with their tri-color flags; and the Prussians have a great double-headed black eagle upon their national flag and on their coat of arms.

They do not take a buzzard, or a hawk, or an ostrich to represent their nation. These birds are large enough, but they haven't got the eagle's noble character, and so this great majestic bird is taken as the symbol or sign of a nation's power. The eagle, like the lion, leads an almost solitary life. It scarcely ever associates with any of its kind, excepting with its mate and its young. He is a very dignified fellow; one that stays at home a good deal, and can not be trifled with. The word for eagle in the Hebrew means the bird that has powerful sight. One of the writers in the Jewish Talmud, or collection of wise sayings, declares that a griffin-eagle, or vulture, at Babylon could see its prey at Jerusalem. I can hardly believe this story, but it is a fact that they can see a great distance, and have a most wonderful eye. They can look straight up at the sun without blinking. This is something no other animal can do. This wonderful eagle-eye can change in a minute from having telescopic power, or power of seeing things at a great distance, to having microscopic power, or the power of seeing things which are very near. For instance, an eagle sees from some great height the body of a dead animal, and instantly swoops down upon it like an arrow from a bow. All this time he is using his telescopic powers; and yet, in a few seconds, when he is close to his prey, the whole form of the eye must be changed, or the bird would mistake its distance and be dashed to pieces on the ground. The eagles build their nests far up on mountain peaks where men would never dare to venture.

There is a place up among the Franconia Mountains, close to the Profile House at the Notch, called "Eagle Cliff," where a number of eagles have their nests and can be seen sailing about in their grand way. From these high nests they take their young out to teach them how to fly, bearing them at first on their wings, until they are strong enough to fly for themselves. This is what the prophet Moses refers to when he says in the book of Deuteronomy, "For the Lord's portion is his people; Jacob is the lot of his inheritance. He found him in a desert land, and in the waste howling wilderness;

he led him about, he instructed him, he kept him as the apple of his eye. As an eagle stirreth up her nest, fluttereth over her young, spreadeth abroad her wings, taketh them, beareth them on her wings; so the Lord alone did lead him, and there was no strange God with him." And then again, in the book of Exodus, he says: "Ye have seen what I did unto the Egyptians, and how I bare you on eagle's wings and brought you unto myself. David says, "Thy youth is renewed like the eagle's," and the prophet Isaiah says, "Even the youths shall faint and be weary, and the young men shall utterly fall: but they that wait upon the Lord shall renew their strength; they shall mount up with wings as eagles; they shall run and not be weary, and they shall walk and not faint." And in the book of Job, where the Lord answered the poor forsaken Job, he says in one place, "Doth the eagle mount up at thy command, and make her nest on high? She dwelleth and abideth on the rock, upon the crag of the rock, and the strong place. From thence she seeketh the prey, and her eyes behold afar off. Her young ones also suck up blood: and where the slain are there is she." Altogether there are thirty places in the Bible where the eagles are mentioned. Altogether the eagle is a very wonderful bird; so that when we come to think of it, we will surely find that the face of the eagle will teach us some important lessons. Well, then, we find in the eagle two kinds of power. And these are:

Power to weather the storms of the world; and power to rise above the storms of the world.

I.

First, then, comes the eagle's power to weather the storms of the world. Did you ever think of what becomes of the birds in the winter-time? Some of them remain all through the winter in their own nests in the trees; some of them, like the little snow-birds, seem to enjoy it all, and they hop about in the snow, as much as to say, "The more snow the more fun." But, then, the greater part of them fly away to the South, as the swallows do, to get away from the storms and cold weather of winter-time. They fly away from the rough weather because they haven't power to stand it. This is the very best thing for them to do; it is an instinct of their nature which teaches them to do this.

Perhaps some of you remember that beautiful song, with the music by the German composer Abt, beginning—

"When the swallows homeward fly."

The wild ducks, too, all along our coast, fly south for the winter. They come along the coast in October and November, and fly away to the Gulf of Mexico and the southern waters, and then in the spring of the year they go back to the coasts of Labrador and Hudson's Bay, to lay their eggs and hatch their young. But the strong eagle never goes south for a milder climate. He stands the stormy weather and the wet and the cold. He clings to the crags of the mountain and makes his nest firm there, among the dwarfed and stumpy pines; and though it snows and hails and sleets up there, and though the piercing winds of winter blow and howl around the bleak mountain, the grand old eagle weathers the storms, and sails in his majestic spiral swoop, round and round, and yet up and up, towards the sun, looking it right in the eye, and poising on its strong and beating wing, as if it did not belong to the earth, but was above it all.

And here it is that we learn our first lesson from the face of the eagle. God has put us into this world, where we are certain and sure to have storms and trouble. And we mustn't run away from the trials and troubles of life; we must learn to weather them; to be able to face them and let them do their worst on us, as the old bald-headed eagle does, when he ruffles his feathers in the mountain rain-storm and makes the best of it, and stretches out his grand old neck to see if he can discover any sign of the sunshine.

The Fourfaced Cherubim. 305

You remember that hymn we sometimes sing—

"We'll stand the storm, it won't be long,
We'll anchor by and by."

And we ought to try to practice these truths we sing, and not merely sing them with our lips.

There are some people who try to run away from the world's care and trouble, by shutting themselves up from the world. They go into monasteries and convents and retreats, and are just like the birds that fly away to the South when the winter is coming on.

Twelve hundred years ago, and after this from time to time in the history of the Christian Church, there were people called hermits, who lived in the rocks, and in cells and caves of the earth. Egypt and the East, and especially along the banks of the river Nile, swarmed with these hermits. Some of them would make vows not to speak to people, for fear they should commit sin; others shut themselves up in caves and dens, and ate nothing but roots and berries. There was one hermit in Italy, named Benedict, who lived in a cave in the side of a rock, and systematically starved himself, until he barely kept the breath in his body. Another one, named Simon Stylites, lived on the top of a tower, and prayed all the time. Now these men were Christians: they thought they were doing God service, and were pleasing Christ by all this kind of life; but they were running away from that very world in which God had placed them. They were not weathering the storms of the world, as the old eagle weathers them; they were simply flying away from them, as the swallows fly away from the storms of winter. There's a certain hymn by Charles Wesley, that wonderful writer of hymns, that has a verse right to this point:

"To the desert or the cell
Let others blindly fly;
In this evil world I dwell;
Nor fear its enmity.

> Here I find a house of prayer
> To which I inwardly retire,
> Walking, unconcerned in care
> And unconsumed in fire."

It is right for us, my dear children, to be in the world, and enjoy its innocent pleasures as well as to suffer its sorrows. God has given us all this faculty for enjoyment: the ringing laugh, the sparkling eye, the sense of fun, and the love of mirth. Why even the animals have this. Who can look at a monkey or a frog without laughing? We have our pleasures as well as our sorrows, and God does not want us to run away from either of them. He wants us to enjoy the sunshine and to weather the storm, not to run away from either of them.

It is these things which will develop us at last, and make us true men and women; for you know we can't be big, grown-up boys and girls, living at home with our parents, and having them do for us all the time. We can't sail in smooth water all the time; we must go out to sea in life some time, we must be built for rough weather. There are a great many people in the world who try to run away from duty, just as the old hermits, I was telling you of, tried hard to run away from the sin in the world by running away from the world altogether. The prophet Jonah was one of these persons. He didn't want to go to Nineveh when God told him to go and preach there. So we read that "Jonah rose up to flee unto Tarshish, from the presence of the Lord, and went down to Joppa; and he found a ship going to Tarshish, so he paid the fare thereof, and went down into it to go with them to Tarshish, from the presence of the Lord."

Well, we all know the rest of the story, and what a hard time he had in trying to run away from duty, instead of standing by and weathering the storm.

There was a young clergyman once, who had a parish where he was doing a great deal of good, and where the people loved him very much. One day, however, he sent in his resignation and left the place. The people tried all they could to get him to remain. The bishop urged him not to go, but he insisted on leaving. And the reason he gave was that there was one queer old man, named Captain Crooks, with whom he could not get on. After this he changed churches six times, and at last, twenty years afterwards, came back to the first church he had. And he said, in explaining it to a young minister,

"Don't run away from duty because there is trouble in the way. I found a Captain Crooks in all six of my churches; he followed me wherever I went, and there was no use in trying to run away from him. He followed me like my own shadow."

And this is all true. We must overcome our difficulties not by running away from them, but by standing our ground and meeting them. We must have the face of the eagle in our lives, and learn to weather the storms of the world. And we can get this power only in one way. We must pray for grace and strength to be able to resist temptation, so that we may be able to *stand*, instead of *running* away, every time we meet with any trouble.

"Who comes there?" cried a French sentinel in the dark.

There was no answer.

"Who comes there!"

Still no reply.

"Who comes there? Stand or give the countersign!" and the lonely picket was relieved in the darkness to hear the well-known, familiar password which showed that it was a friend. Presently a muffled form approached, and the sentinel found that it was no less a person than General Bonaparte, the young French leader of the army in Italy. He had had some reason to doubt about certain of his sentinels, and so in the darkness and silence of the night he was going the rounds, testing the strength and courage of the pickets. And that was the way that Napoleon Bonaparte received the name among his soldiers of "The Little Corporal."

Well, my dear children, if we are trying to be God's faithful soldiers and servants unto our life's end, we are like sentinels in the dark. We can not see very much before us; the light of the morning has not come yet, and it is required in us that we be found faithful. We must stand our ground, and face our duties, trials, and responsibilities; we will be traitors if we throw down our arms and fly.

Power to weather the storms of the world. This is the first thing the face of the eagle teaches us.

II.

The second kind of power the face of the eagle teaches us is, power to rise above the storms of the world.

The eagle can fly higher in the air, and can sustain itself longer on its strong and tireless wing, than any of the other birds. It never gets dizzy away up in its soaring. It is at home up there; and though at times it flies so very far away that we can not see it, still it knows that higher world perfectly well, and comes back from its flights to its old home in the rocks, just as surely and as safely as the swallows come back to their nests, after skimming along on the surface of the lake. And just in the same way, as if on eagles' wings, on the rising, beating stroke of faith and hope, the Christian ought to be able to rise up above the storms of the world higher than any other kind of man.

In the old pictures of the Evangelists, as we have already seen, St. Matthew is always represented with a cherub or human face by his side, St. Mark with a lion, St. Luke with an ox, and St. John with an eagle. These are the same four faces of the cherubim which Ezekiel saw in his vision. It means that every form of life was in that eternal life which Jesus Christ our Saviour has given to us through the gospel; it means that the Evangelists represented to us every form of life in Jesus, and that in heaven, among all the angels and redeemed, all that was best and strongest in this life would be there.

The reason why St. John is always represented with an eagle is, simply because he soared higher up into the light and knowledge of God than the other disciples. He loved Jesus more than any of the others, and so it seemed to him as if his Saviour loved him more; and he was known as the disciple whom Jesus loved. And if we are true Christians and followers of God as true children, we ought to be able to get up into God's light, and away from the troubles of the world, just as the eagle gets up at times above the clouds: so that while it is raining upon the poor little birds who fly low and keep near the earth, he, because of his power to rise above the storms of the world, goes wheeling about in his slow, grand way, where it is all sunshine.

I suppose the little birds can't imagine what the eagle is up to when he goes off for a flight. No doubt they wonder and wonder how he lives up there and what he is about.

Here is a fable in rhyme about an owl and an eagle:

" The eagle thought to explore the skies,
  The owl vouchsafed him counsel wise:
  ' Give up this profitless waste of wing,
  Keep close to me, I'll teach you to sing.
  All creatures are sure to lose their senses,
  If they venture above the trees and fences:
  I knew of a foolhardy, crazy lark,
  Which flew away up and was lost in the dark.
  You can't go up any higher than I,
  Nothing to roost on; fool to try;
  You'll bump your head against the sky.
  Sit still till the horrible day is done,
  No one can see till the shade is on;
  The sun is a cloud and the moon is a sun.'
  (The eagle sailing the upper sea,
  Did he hear his friend's soliloquy?)

" ' He has lost his hold! He floats in despair
  On the frightful space of the empty air!
  If a flash of darkness would let him see,
  He might find his way again back to me.
  But he's out of sight, and therefore lost,
  And in the abyss by wild winds is tossed.

I told him better! The rattle-brains
Will find that liberty ends in chains.
Had he sense enough to take advice,
He might have been useful—catching mice.
Do you hear him scream? 'Tis the cry of distress,
As he gyrates downward; a pretty mess
Will his carcass make as he strikes the stones!
But, never mind, I'll pick his bones!"

But the eagle wouldn't care for all this small talk from an owl in the dark; he lives in a higher world; he has other things to think of; he has a certain kind of power the owl hasn't got: it is the power to rise above the storms of the world.

And this kind of power in the soul is what the Christian has got, and the man who isn't a Christian hasn't got. The Christian prays to God, and communes with his Saviour, and lives in the thoughts of heaven and the life everlasting. The man who don't believe in God, or the hereafter, and who doubts whether he has got any soul, is just like the owl in the dark. He wants to keep down on the roosts and fences, and grub about in the earth; he doesn't rise one bit above the things of this world. Look at St. Paul and then look at the emperor Nero. The one lived far above the world, like the eagle, and the other lived down in the dark, like the owl.

St. Paul was not afraid of any thing: he faced angry mobs and crowds, and was in danger of death all the time; but he said that none of these things moved him, and that he even did not count his life dear unto him, so that he finish his work for his divine Master with joy. When the crowd of angry Jews at Jerusalem tried to kill him, and had bound themselves by an oath not to eat or drink until they had done this thing, as he looked out upon that sea of upturned angry faces, breathing out threatenings and death against him, with the Roman soldiers having all they could do to keep him from being torn in pieces,—I tell you, my dear children, this man had the face of the eagle in his life, as he rose above it all and said, "What if they do kill my body; not one of them can touch my soul." And we read that that very night the Lord stood by him and said, "Be of good cheer, Paul; for as thou hast testified of me in Jerusalem, so must thou bear witness also at Rome."

Do you suppose he was afraid of any thing when he felt that his Lord, who had been all through this same kind of persecution, was standing by him?

And then, see him again in the terrible storm they had in the Mediterranean. For fourteen days the ship was tossed up and down in the tempest, and the sailors and soldiers on board did not know what to do. Some of the cowardly sailors, or "shipmen," as St. Paul called them, tried to make off in the boats and desert the ship, as we have seen in a former sermon. And then St. Paul, though he was a prisoner bound with a chain, and on his way to the judgment-seat of the emperor Nero, stood up above them all, and cheered them all to be brave men, saying: "And now I exhort you to be of good cheer: for there shall be no loss of any man's life among you, but of the ship. For there stood by me this night the angel of God, whose I am and whom I serve, saying, fear not Paul; thou must be brought before Cæsar: and lo, God hath given thee all them that sail with thee. Wherefore, sirs, be of good cheer: for I believe God, that it shall be even as it was told me."

Didn't St. Paul have the face of an eagle at such times as these, when he rose up above all his companions, just as the eagle, king among birds, sweeps up into regions where no other birds can follow?

Now look at the emperor Nero; the man before whom St. Paul was to stand and be tried. He didn't believe in any God, or any hereafter. He was a cruel-hearted wretch, and lived in constant fear of death. He burned Rome, and then played the violin while it was burning, and laid the blame of the conflagration upon the poor innocent Christians. He hated his own mother Agrippina, and sent her off on a pleasant yachting excursion, and then gave secret orders to the sailors to sink the boat and drown her, because she was in his way. But he didn't succeed in this, for Agrippina didn't drown as easily as was expected, and managed some how to swim ashore. At last the legions of the Roman army became tired of Nero's cruelties, and they raised a revolt, and bribed the slaves in the palace to kill him. Nero heard of it in some way and tried to escape. He ran out into the garden of his palace, and thought he was safely hidden in some of the bushes. But the slaves dragged him out, and while he crouched before them, and rolled on the ground, begging for his life, they held him and stabbed him to death, just as men kill a mad dog. No face of the eagle there! No rising above the storms of the world there! Oh what that wretched man would have given for something of that brave apostle's faith, the man Paul, whom he condemned to be put to death!

Power to weather the storms of the world; power to rise above the storms of the world.

These are the two kinds of power the face of the eagle teaches us. We will need them both in trying to serve Christ, and do our duty to him and to our fellow-men. We will need the first kind of power while we are living. We will need the second kind of power when the time comes for us to die.

Dear children, pray to God to give you these two kinds of power: Power to resist evil. Power to rise above it.

May you indeed "fight manfully against the world, the flesh, and the devil, and continue Christ's faithful soldiers and servants unto your life's end! Amen."

XII.

The Fourfaced Cherubim.

No. 4.—THE FACE OF A MAN.

THE FOURFACED CHERUBIM.

IV. THE FACE OF A MAN.

"The face of a man."—EZEKIEL i. 10.

THIS is the fourth and last sermon about the wonderful cherubim.

You know in that beautiful hymn of praise called the "Te Deum," beginning—

"We praise Thee, O God; we acknowledge Thee to be the Lord,"

there are these words:

"To Thee cherubim and seraphim continually do cry, "Holy, Holy, Holy, Lord God of Sabaoth."

Now these cherubim and seraphim are wonderful living beings. But it is very doubtful if they are angels, as we understand that word. Angels are messengers, single-faced spirits, heavenly sons of God. But all through the Bible, from the cherubim with flaming swords who kept the gate of Eden, after Adam was driven from it, as described in the book of Genesis, all the way down to the "beasts," or "living creatures," which were before the throne of God as St. John describes them in the book of the Revelation, these cherubim are spoken of as wonderful living beings, with all forms of life in them; they are not angels, with only one face or form to them.

We have seen three of these faces or forms of life: the face of a lion, the face of an ox, and the face of an eagle. To-day we come to the last of them all—the highest and the best—"The face of a man."

The face of a man, then, shows us two kinds of knowledge, or two kinds of power,—for knowledge is power,—and these are:

The power of knowing ourselves, and the power of knowing God.

I.

First of all, is this power of knowing ourselves.

A looking-glass is a very wonderful thing. It shows us ourselves, and just the way we appear to others. There are some glasses which show us the back of our heads, and our side faces, so that we can see ourselves all the way round. But we forget how we appear to others; we don't remember what we are like. This is what St. James has in mind when he says: "If any be a hearer of the word, and not a doer, he is like unto a man beholding his natural face in a glass: for he beholdeth himself, and goeth his way, and straightway forgetteth what manner of man he was."

I knew a gentleman, once, who hunted all over the house to find his spectacles. He looked in his table and desk, and all through the pockets of his different clothes, but couldn't find them in any place. At last he called his servant.

"John," said he, "have you seen my glasses anywhere?"

"Yes," replied John, "I see them this very minute."

"Where are they?" he inquired.

"On your nose, sir," said John.

Now, if that gentleman had only beheld himself once in the glass, if he had only had the power of knowing himself, if he had seen his own face,—the face of a man, —he would not have been compelled to hunt by the hour for his missing spectacles.

How very few of us there are who really know what we are like. There is an old Greek motto which has come to us from the time of Plato, the great philosopher of Greece, containing these two short words: 'Γνωϑί ϭεαυτον," "Know thyself." This is, a most important branch of knowledge, this knowing ourselves. You know there are some people who are called phrenologists: they believe that a person's character can be told by examining the bumps on his head. As you go into the office of a phrenologist you will see a bust of a human head, with all the different bumps marked on it, and underneath the head you will see this motto, "Know thyself." These phrenologists think that people do not know themselves until they have had their heads examined and have received a character-book.

When I was a boy in college I went to a phrenologist's office, and the man rubbed his fingers through my hair, and called out a lot of numbers, which a clerk put down in a book; and then, when I left, this book was given to me; and there were a great many things in it that were very true. One thing I remember was, that I didn't like mathematics, and had no turn for all those hard problems in algebra and geometry; and that was just like looking in the glass and seeing what manner of man I was.

But there are a great many people in the world who never have any knowledge of themselves, even if they do go to a phrenologist's and get a character-book. You know there are some old Scotch lines by the poet Burns, which read—

> "Oh wad some power the giftie gie us
> To see oursel's as others see us."

These people think of themselves as they appear to themselves, not at all as they appear to others. Sometimes, when boys go to school, and especially when they go away to boarding-school, they have a hard time in finding their proper places. I remember a boy at school who always tried to boss it over us little fellows by saying, "Don't you know who I am? I am Mr. ——'s son!"

At last the other boys made up their minds they would stand it no longer, and they took him off in the woods, just as Indians carry off a captive to torture, and then they tied his feet and hands, and made a paddle out of a shingle, and gave him a terrible dressing down; and after that the big braggart found his place, and began to have the face of a man in his character. He began to know himself.

Animals haven't got this power of knowing themselves. A horse can tell another horse from a dog, or a cow, and yet he doesn't stop to think how it is that he is a horse. He don't know any thing about his own nature. He knows he likes oats, and he knows he loves to roll in a field; but he doesn't stop to think that a horse is a common noun, or that his name is spelt, h—o—r—s—e, or how the sentence "*I am a horse*" is to be parsed. He has no power of knowing himself.

A horse has the face, or the character, of a horse; and a dog has the face, or character, of a dog: that is, they have all the powers which belong to horses and dogs; but they never can get the face, or the character, of a man in their lives. They have nothing of this twofold knowledge which man has, this power of knowing ourselves, and this power of knowing God.

And this power,—this face of a man in our lives,—comes to us slowly and by degrees. We are not born with it all at once.

Look, for instance, at a little baby. It knows nothing at all when it is born. But as it grows up to be a little child it begins to learn things. It picks up words; then the child knows father and mother and nurse and doctor, long before it can spell these words, or parse in grammar the sentences it speaks. All this knowledge comes afterwards. It don't have to wait until it knows every thing about itself, before it begins to love those about it, or know right from wrong. Solomon says, "Even a child is known by its doings,"—long before it can understand all about those doings. But by and by this knowledge comes, and then the face of the man appears, with its knowledge of itself and with its knowledge of God.

What is it then truly to know ourselves?

Well, it means a great many things. First we learn about our wonderful body, this strange house of flesh and bone that we live in. We learn, or ought to learn, the laws of health: how to dress ourselves rightly in summer and winter, what to eat, and how to keep well. Then we have the whole world to learn about, and how it is that we are inhabitants of the world. Then we have our mind to train up in the right way, so as to let it learn how to think and work rightly. The understanding is like the foundation of the house, and the memory is like the walls; and looking out upon life for ourselves, is like the windows of the house. Then we have to learn about another side to our nature,—the moral side. We ought to know right from wrong when we see them, just as we can tell a bird from a snake. We ought to feel our cheeks burn red with shame when we do any thing wrong, or mean, or selfish. *That is God's hand in our blood which reddens it so.* It is the conscience that keeps the score when we do right and when we do wrong, and calls out like a scorer on a baseball field, "Right! Wrong!"

And above all these,—above the mind, and the moral sense,—you and I have a soul,—an immortal spirit,—something that will not die at death, but will live beyond; something which we ought to preserve from sin and evil; something which Jesus came to save.

So you see, after all, we are like this wonderful cherubim itself. We have four faces, or sides, to our being: the face, or the side, of the body; the side of the mind; the side of the moral sense, and the side of the immortal spirit. And so, too, we are four-sided, and are very much like this cherubim after all. The face of the man, then, is very far above the other faces which we have been talking about, because we read in the book of Genesis that man was made in the image of God, and none of the other living creatures were made after this likeness.

When we are little children we love to see and be with animals. We love to talk about them, and have picture-books with animals in them, and play with menageries and farms. It seems as if we belong to them and they to us; as if we were all brothers and sisters. How a boy loves his pigeons and rabbits and guinea pigs, and the funny little puppies that tumble about so, and try

The Fourfaced Cherubim. 333

to bite before they have any teeth, and put on such big airs! How a little girl loves her little kittens! How she mauls them, and picks the old mother cat up any how, just as you pick up a pillow, in any place where it is soft! And all this natural love of animals comes out of our animal life. When we are little we haven't got the face of the man developed within us, we haven't come to our full power, and therefore the life that the animals lead seems to be our life, and we feel that we are one with them.

But the power of truly knowing ourselves consists in something more than finding out how much better our nature is than that of the animal world. We may know all about our bodies: all about the world we live in, and the laws by which it is governed. We may know all about our own minds, and be able to explain just how it is that we exist as living beings, and yet we may never know ourselves as God knows us: for we are told that "man looketh upon the outward appearance, but the Lord looketh upon the heart."

There is something wrong in the soul; there is a hidden fire there that bursts out from time to time into a flame; there is a disease in the soul that is called sin; and sin in the soul makes us sinners, just as sickness in the body makes us sick. A man who is sick must know that he is sick, before he can take any thing that will make him well. And we, my dear children, must find out that we are sinners, before we can truly know ourselves, or can know God, or his great medicine for us. And to have the face of a man and know ourselves truly, we must find out that we need a Saviour; and when we have found this out, we are ready for the second kind of knowledge which this face of a man teaches us.

II.

Power of knowing God, is the other kind of power the face of a man has. The animals, as we have seen, know very little about themselves or about the world they live in. They know when they are hungry, and some of them have a great deal of instinct, as it is called, or the power of knowing what to do to bring up their young and take care of themselves. The beavers know how to build dams and make their houses by the waterside. Birds know how to build their nests, and hens know that they must sit on their eggs and keep them warm, if they want to have a brood of little chickens. They don't have to go to school, or college, to learn these things. The great Creator has given them all this knowledge. We call it instinct. But that is the end of it. They have no sense of sin, excepting as trained animals are taught that they will be whipped unless they do as they are told.

There was a little fellow once who had some canary-birds, which were great pets. He used to watch them a great deal, and would let them out to fly about the room, and they would come on his finger and eat hemp-seed out of his mouth. One day, after he had been watching them drink out of their trough, he said to his mother,

"Mother, don't you think my canary-birds will surely go to heaven when they die?"

"Why, my dear?" replied his mother. "What makes you think that they will?"

"Oh," said the little fellow, "because they are so pious, mother. I never saw any birds that were so religious."

"Pious!" she said, "pious birds! What do they do that is pious?"

"Oh, mother," he answered, "you ought to see them when they drink. Every time they put their beaks down into the water, they lift their heads up and look right up into the sky, as much as to say, 'For what we have received, oh Lord, make us truly thankful.' They do it every time, and *I* think they really do say grace to themselves every time they drink. Yes, mother, I am sure my birds are pious, for they look as if they returned thanks to God, just as father does before soup."

This was a pretty thought that the little boy had about his birds. But these birds had only the face, or the character, of the birds in their nature; they didn't have the face of a man, with its power of knowing God.

But how do we know God? how do we feel him? What does it all mean?

Let us see. We have never seen God, and yet among all the races of the earth, among all the nations that have been and are to-day, we find this universal belief in God. And even those people who are heathen and have no knowledge of the true God, yet have made for themselves idols or images of God, as we say in that hymn by Bishop Heber,

> "The heathen in their blindness
> Bow down to wood and stone."

But we, who are Christians, have no idols or images of God. The second commandment tells us we are not to make to ourselves graven images, and are not to worship them, as in any way representing God to us.

We come to God through our Lord Jesus Christ, our Saviour, who came in our flesh; and thus when we think of him, or see him, in our mind's eye, we think of God and see God.

We read in the first chapter of St. John's gospel, at the eighteenth verse, these words: "No man hath seen God at any time; the only begotten Son, which is in the bosom of the Father, he hath declared him."

When he was upon Mount Sinai Moses asked God to show him his glory. But we are told that God said to him that he could not see his full glory and live. And then God revealed something of his presence to his servant, and the face of Moses shone with the brightness of the place.

And when Jesus was upon earth, one of the disciples said unto him, "Lord show us the Father, and it sufficeth us." That is, he meant to say, show us something of God in his glory in heaven and we won't ask for any thing more; that will do; then we will be sure to believe. And then our Lord replied by saying, "Have I been so long time with you, and yet hast thou not known me, Philip? He that hath seen me hath seen the Father; and how sayest thou then, show us the Father." That is, Jesus meant to tell his disciples that they couldn't see God with the eyes of their body; but they could see him who was God in the flesh, God who became man.

For instance, look at a thunder storm. You hear the thunder rolling in the heavens, you feel the air growing cold, you see the sky growing dark; there seems to be a silence, when, all of a sudden, a crash comes, and the lightning flashes through the clouds, and strikes some old oak-tree. But the electric fluid which caused that lightning was up in the clouds all the time. It didn't come merely when the lightning came, it was there before; but the lightning revealed the electricity, it declared that which already was in the bosom of the clouds. So God revealed himself amid the thunders of Mount Sinai, when he gave the Jewish people their law. That was a visible manifestation of God's power. Again he revealed himself, again the lightning was seen, when Jesus, at his baptism, was declared to be the only son in whom God the Father was well pleased. Again the lightning was seen, at the day of Pentecost, when there appeared cloven tongues, as of fire, upon the heads of the apostles, and the place in which they were sitting was filled with the clouds of God's glory.

You know in St. John's gospel he begins by telling us that Jesus Christ was the Word of God. "In the beginning was the Word, and the Word was with God, and the Word was God."

Just think for a moment what a word is!

A class in school were gathered together, once, around the teacher's desk. She had lost the key of her money-drawer. Some one either had taken it, or knew where it was. Every boy and girl must say yes, or no; must tell a lie, or tell the truth. That teacher and the other boys and girls did not know what thoughts were in the minds of that class standing up before the desk. Each scholar might have falsehood or truth in his mind. No one could tell what the thoughts were, until the word yes, or no, was spoken, and then the word revealed the mind. And words always reveal our thoughts; they are our thoughts spoken out to the world.

And so St. John says that Jesus is the *word* of God. He is God's thought, seen in the world; he reveals the mind of God: for God is truth, God is love, and Jesus Christ is the revelation of God's truth and love. Jesus is the spoken word "*yes*," to God's thoughts of love for us.

My dear children, we may be able to know God in many ways.

First of all, we can see God in his works. You remember in the story of Robinson Crusoe, how, one day, while he was roaming over his island with his parrot on his shoulder and his big umbrella over him, all of a sudden, there, right before him on the sand, was the print of a human foot. What did that mean? what did that prove? of what was that the evidence? Why it proved to him that somebody else was on his desert island; that he was not alone there. And you know in a little while after he found poor Friday.

Now, suppose Robinson had found, a little further on, a compass and a barometer on the sand. How did these come there?

"Oh," says Friday, "I guess they just happened to come there; they dropped from some of the clouds, or perhaps they grew there."

"No," says Robinson, "that's all nonsense; they were made; they were designed by a man; don't you see all the wheels and screws and pivots; some workman planned them, and made them in a shop, and they've been washed ashore from some sinking ship."

Well, my dear children, we are just like Robinson and Friday on the sand. We see marks of a divine hand, footprints of some great power here in the world. The blue sky, the green grass, summer and winter, coal and food, water and air, fire and storm, sun and moon, oceans and seas, cattle and living things,—all show us the marks of design. They were created for a purpose, as the compass and barometer were made in a shop; they didn't merely happen to come here in this world from some unknown cause, or grow up out of nothing, as Friday said the compass grew up out of the beach.

And this knowledge of God which comes from looking at his works, is what Shadrach, Meshach, and Abed-nego had, when they sang in the midst of the fiery furnace that chant called the "Benedicite," which we sing sometimes in our churches. "O all ye works of the Lord, bless ye the Lord; praise him, and magnify him forever:

"O ye stars of heaven, oh ye winds of God, oh ye mountains and hills, bless ye the Lord; praise him, and magnify him forever."

Then we know God again by the conscience within us. If you have ever been up in an organ-loft, and have seen a man blow the organ there, you will find a little piece of wood that slides up and down a groove. It is called a "telltale." It is connected with the bellows by a string, and it goes up and down with the bellows, and tells the blower when he can stop blowing, and when he must go on again. So there is something within us which is like this telltale. Something speaks out when we do right and says "yes"; and something speaks out and says "no," when we do wrong. St. Paul says, in one place, that the law of God is written *in the heart;* just as you can write your name in the sand on the beach with a sharp stick. This conscience that we have is like the thermometer: it tells us how warm or how cold our sense of duty is. It is like the barometer in the cabin of a ship: it will tell us when the sky is clear, and when a storm is coming.

And then, last of all, we know God by the written word which he has given us, the revelation of his will from heaven. "Search the Scriptures," said Jesus once to the Jews, "for these are they which testify of me." This Bible is the word of life. It is the record of holy men, who spake as they were moved by the Spirit of God. It all points to

Jesus Christ as the central fact and hope of the world, and tells us the Son of man came to seek and to save that which was lost.

And thus, by the world of nature, and by our conscience, and by the Word of God, with its revelation of Jesus Christ, we are able to have this wonderful face of a man in our lives, and are able to know God.

Power of knowing ourselves.
Power of knowing God.

These are the two kinds of power the face of a man teaches us.

When we know ourselves best, then we will feel that we are weak and sinful; and when we truly know God, we will know that he is strong, and that he is made for us to rest our souls upon him.

Thank God, then, my dear children, that you have got this wonderful face of a man in your characters.

The face of a lion taught us the lessons of activity and courage; the face of the ox taught us the power of doing and of suffering; the face of the eagle taught us the lesson of weathering the storms of the world and of getting above the storms of the world; but the face of a man, crowning all the other faces of this wonderful thing of life,—this mysterious cherubim,—is better than all the others, as it teaches us that we have the power of knowing ourselves, and the power of knowing God.

Pray to God, then, that he may teach you truly to know your own heart, that you may know both yourself and Christ your Saviour.

For, as St. John says in closing his first epistle, "We know that the Son of God is come, and hath given us an understanding, that we may know him that is true; and we are in him that is true, even in his Son Jesus Christ. This is the true God and eternal life. Little children, keep yourselves from idols. Amen."

THE END.

530 Broadway, New York,
October, 1878.

Robert Carter & Brothers'
NEW BOOKS.

LITTLE LIGHTS ALONG SHORE. By Paul Cobden. 9 illustrations. 16mo. $1.25.

HOME LESSONS ON THE OLD PATHS; OR, CONVERSATIONS ON THE SHORTER CATECHISM. 9 illustrations. 16mo. $1.25.

THE WIDOW'S TRUST. By Mrs. Martha T. Gale. (Little Classic Style.)

JOHN, WHOM JESUS LOVED. By Dr. Culross. 12mo. $1.25.

THEOLOGICAL LECTURES. By the late Principal Cunningham. 8vo. $3.00.

D'AUBIGNÉ'S HISTORY OF THE REFORMATION IN THE TIME OF CALVIN. Vol. VIII. (Completing the work.) $2.00.
　The set in 8 volumes. $16.00.

D'AUBIGNÉ'S HISTORY OF THE REFORMATION IN THE SIXTEENTH CENTURY. 5 vols. $6.00.

MARGERY'S SON. By Miss Holt. $1.50.

By Miss L. T. Meade.
DAVID'S LITTLE LAD. 12mo. $1.25.
SCAMP AND I. 12mo. $1.25.
A KNIGHT OF TO-DAY. 12mo. $1.50.
Several new volumes by this gifted lady are in active preparation, to be issued during the Autumn.

SPRINGDALE SERIES. 6 vols., each with a colored frontispiece and colored picture on the cover. In a box. $2.00.

THE TASK. By William Cowper. Illustrated by Birket Foster. A truly elegant book. $3.50.

SERMONS BY THE REV. J. OSWALD DYKES, D.D., of Regent's Square, London.

ROSE BARTON'S MISTAKE. By Mrs. Dodds (Daughter of Dr. Horatius Bonar). 16mo.

THE KING IN HIS BEAUTY. By the Rev. Richard Newton, D.D., Author of the "Jewel Case," "Wonder Case," &c. 16mo. 6 illustrations. $1.25.

BEAUTY FOR ASHES. By Rev. Alexander Dickson, Author of "All about Jesus." 12mo. $2.00.

THE OLD LOOKING-GLASS; or, Dorothy Cope's Recollections. By the Author of "Ministering Children." 4 illustrations. $1.00.

By the Author of
"THE WIDE WIDE WORLD."

THE BROKEN WALLS. 16mo. $1.25.

THE KINGDOM OF JUDAH. 16mo. $1.50.

THE KING'S PEOPLE. Comprising —

WALKS FROM EDEN.	STAR OUT OF JACOB.
HOUSE OF ISRAEL.	KINGDOM OF JUDAH.
THE BROKEN WALLS.	

5 vols. *In a box.* $7.00.

By the same Author.

SMALL BEGINNINGS. 4 vols. . . $5.00 | THE SAY AND DO SERIES. 6
THE OLD HELMET . . . . . 2.25 | vols. $7.50
MELBOURNE HOUSE. . . . . 2.00 | PINE NEEDLES 1.50

POINTED PAPERS FOR THE CHRISTIAN LIFE. By the Rev. T. L. CUYLER. 12mo. $1.50.

EVENTIDE AT BETHEL. By MACDUFF. $1.25.

DR. HODGES'S OUTLINES OF THEOLOGY.
New edition, rewritten and enlarged. 8vo. $3.00.

ABRAHAM, THE FRIEND OF GOD. By the Rev. J. OSWALD DYKES, D.D. $1.50.

THE HIDDEN LIFE. By the Rev. PHILIP SAPHIR. 12mo. $1.50.

THE HOUSE IN THE GLEN AND THE BOYS WHO BUILT IT. $1.25.

THE PERSON OF CHRIST. By the Rev. ANDREW A. BONAR. 18mo. 50 cents.

TAKE CARE OF No. 1. By the Rev. P. B. POWER
9 illustrations. 16mo. $1.00.

BRIGHTER THAN THE SUN. A Life of our Lord. By J. R. MACDUFF, D.D. With 16 full-page illustrations by ROWAN. Printed on superfine paper, and elegantly bound. $2 00.

AMONG THE TURKS. By CYRUS HAMLIN, D.D. 12mo. $1.50.

THE CHRISTIAN HERITAGE, and other Sermons. By the late MELANCTHON W. JACOBUS, D.D. A Memorial Volume with Portrait. 12mo. $1.50.

AUTOBIOGRAPHY OF THE REV. WILLIAM ARNOT. And Memoir by his Daughter, Mrs. FLEMING. $2.00.

JACK O'LANTERN. A delightful book for little children. 9 illustrations. 16mo. $1.25.

THE PEEP OF DAY LIBRARY. 8 vols. 18mo. In a box. $4.50.

OLIVER OF THE MILL. By the Author of "Ministering Children." 12mo. $1.50.

A PEEP BEHIND THE SCENES. By Mrs. WALTON, Author of "Christie's Old Organ." $1.25.

CHRISTIE'S OLD ORGAN. 50 cents.

MOORE'S FORGE. A Tale. By the Author of "Win and Wear." $1.25.

By the same Author.

WIN AND WEAR SERIES. 6 vols. $7.50
THE GREEN MOUNTAIN STORIES. 5 vols. 6.00

LEDGESIDE SERIES. 6 vols. . $7.50
BUTTERFLY'S FLIGHTS. 3 vols. 2.25
HIGHLAND SERIES. 6 vols. . 7.50

THE FOOTSTEPS OF ST. PETER. By J. R. MACDUFF, D.D., Author of the "Footsteps of St. Paul." $2.00.

LETTICE EDEN. By EMILY SARAH HOLT. $1.50.

By the same Authors.

ISOULT BARRY. 12mo. . . . $1.50	VERENA. 12mo $1.50
ROBIN TREMAYNE. 12mo. . . 1.50	THE WHITE ROSE OF LANGLEY 1.50
THE WELL IN THE DESERT . 1.25	IMOGEN. 12mo 1.50
ASHCLIFFE HALL. 16mo. . . 1.25	CLARE AVERY. 12mo. . . . 1.50

MILLY'S WHIMS. By JOANNA H. MATHEWS, Author of the "Bessie Books," &c. 16mo. $1.25.

HAPS AND MISHAPS. By the Misses MATHEWS. 6 vols. 16mo. In a box. $7.50. Containing:—

LITTLE FRIENDS OF GLENWOOD $1.25	MILLY'S WHIMS $1.25
THE BROKEN MALLET . . . 1.25	UNCLE JOE'S THANKSGIVING . 1.25
BLACKBERRY JAM 1.25	LILIES OR THISTLEDOWN . . 1.25

By the same Authors.

THE BESSIE BOOKS. 6 vols. . $7.50	KITTY AND LULU BOOKS. 6 vols. $6.00
THE FLOWERETS. 6 vols. . . 3.60	MISS ASHTON'S GIRLS. 6 vols. 7.50
LITTLE SUNBEAMS. 6 vols. . 6.00	

LILIES OR THISTLEDOWN. A Tale. By JULIA A. MATHEWS. $1.25.

UNCLE JOE'S THANKSGIVING. $1.25.

By the same Author.

GOLDEN LADDER SERIES. 6 vols. $3.00	DARE TO DO RIGHT SERIES . $5.50
DRAYTON HALL SERIES. 6 vols. 4.50	KATY AND JIM 1.25

LITTLE AND WISE. By Rev. W. W. NEWTON. 16mo. $1.25.

SERVANTS OF CHRIST. 18mo. 50 cents.

HERO IN THE BATTLE OF LIFE. 18mo. 50 cts.

BIBLE ECHOES. By Rev. JAMES WELLS. $1.25.

FIGHTING THE FOE. 12mo. $1.50.

RAYS FROM THE SUN OF RIGHTEOUSNESS.
By Rev. RICHARD NEWTON, D.D. Illustrated. $1.25.

THE WONDER CASE. By the Rev. R. NEWTON, D.D. Containing:—

BIBLE WONDERS $1.25	LEAVES FROM TREE OF LIFE . $1.25
NATURE'S WONDERS 1.25	RILLS FROM FOUNTAIN . . . 1.25
JEWISH TABERNACLE 1.25	GIANTS AND WONDERS . . . 1.25

6 vols. *In a box.* $7.50.

THE JEWEL CASE. By the Same. 6 vols. In a box. $7.50.

THE A. L. O. E. LIBRARY. 55 vols. In a neat Wooden Case, walnut trimmings. $40.00.

New A. L. O. E. Books.

INDIAN STORIES. 18mo. 75 cents.

THE HAUNTED ROOMS. 16mo, $1.25; 18mo, 75 cents.

THE TINY RED NIGHT-CAP. 50 cents.

FRITZ'S VICTORY. 50 cents.

THE TRUANT KITTEN. 50 cents.

VICTORY STORIES. Containing the last three. 16mo. $1.25.

HEROES OF ISRAEL. 5 vols. 16mo. $5.00.

www.ingramcontent.com/pod-product-compliance
Lightning Source LLC
Chambersburg PA
CBHW032354230426
43672CB00007B/702